Max Wright was born in County Down in 1932. He was educated at Campbell College and Queen's University Belfast, from where he graduated with a BA in Philosophy. He was also awarded a Ph.D. by the Australian National University, Canberra. He currently lives in Belfast, where he lectures in Philosophy at Queen's University.

Told in Gath

MAX WRIGHT

THE
BLACKSTAFF
PRESS

BELFAST

ACKNOWLEDGEMENTS

Copyright material from the following is acknowledged: W.H. Auden, 'In Memory of W.B. Yeats' and '1st September 1939' in *Collected Shorter Poems 1930–1944*, London, Faber and Faber, 1950; J.L. Austin, *Philosophical Papers*, Oxford, Clarendon Press, 1961; Patricia Beer, *Mrs Beer's House*, London, Macmillan, 1968; Cyril Connolly, *The Unquiet Grave*, London, Hamish Hamilton, 1945; T.S. Eliot, *The Cocktail Party*, London, Faber and Faber, 1950, and 'The Hippopotamus' and 'Choruses from The Rock' in *Collected Poems 1909–1935*, London, Faber and Faber, 1936; Graham Greene, *The Lawless Roads*, London, Longman, Green and Co., 1939, and *Brighton Rock*, London, William Heinemann, 1938; Christopher Isherwood, *Goodbye to Berlin*, London, The Hogarth Press, 1939; James Joyce, *Stephen Hero*, London, Jonathan Cape, 1944, and *Ulysses*, London, The Bodley Head, 1937; Stanislaus Joyce, *My Brother's Keeper*, London, Faber and Faber, 1958; George Orwell, 'Inside the Whale', an essay in *England, your England and Other Essays*, London, Martin Secker and Warburg, 1953; V.S. Pritchett, *The Living Novel*, London, Chatto and Windus, 1964; Forrest Reid, *Peter Waring*, London, Faber and Faber, 1937; Evelyn Waugh, *The Diaries of Evelyn Waugh*, ed. Michael Davie, London, Weidenfeld and Nicolson, 1976; Simone Weil, *Waiting on God*, London, Routledge and Kegan Paul, 1951; Thornton Wilder, *Heaven's my Destination*, London, Longman, Green and Co., 1934; L. Wittgenstein, *Philosophical Investigations*, Oxford, Basil Blackwell, 1953.

First published in 1990 by
The Blackstaff Press Limited
3 Galway Park, Dundonald, Belfast BT16 0AN, Northern Ireland
with the assistance of
The Arts Council of Northern Ireland

Typeset by Textflow Services Limited

Printed by The Guernsey Press Company Limited

British Library Cataloguing in Publication Data
Wright, Max
Told in Gath.
1. Biographies
I. Title
191

ISBN 0-85640-449-7 (hardback)
0-85640-439-X (paperback)

for my granddaughters
Claire and Rachel

Tell it not in Gath,
publish it not in the streets of Askelon;
lest the daughters of the Philistines rejoice ...

2 Samuel 1: 20

Lord with what care hast thou begirt us round!
Parents first season us; then schoolmasters
Deliver us to laws; they send us, bound
To rules of reason, holy messengers,

Pulpits and sundayes, sorrow dogging sinne,
Afflictions sorted, anguish of all sizes,
Fine nets and stratagems to catch us in,
Bibles laid open, millions of surprises,

Blessings beforehand, tyes of gratefulnesse,
The sound of glorie ringing in our eares;
Without, our shame; within, our consciences;
Angels and grace, eternall hopes and fears

Yet all these fences and their whole array
One cunning bosom-sinne blows quite away.

George Herbert

INTRODUCTION

DR FRED STANLEY ARNOTT STEVENSON, MB, BCh., BAO

I was born in the same week in March 1932 as the author of this book, and grew up with him in the years before the Second World War in the seaside town of Bangor, County Down. We both had the great privilege of being born into a Christian home, our parents having been saved many years before we were born. I was the youngest of a family of six, while the author was an only child. In those happy days before the war we swam together at Pickie Pool and played in Strickland's Glen which was near my home or in the then undeveloped fields at Broadway, close to where he lived. We were in the same class both at the Sunday school in the gospel hall at Central Avenue and at the public elementary school.

Then in 1941 a great tragedy occurred. In the aftermath of the Easter Tuesday blitz on Belfast, two bombs fell on our quiet town. One of them scored a direct hit on the author's home. His father was killed and his mother lost one of her legs and suffered such great injuries to the other that although it was saved, for the rest of her life she was much more severely crippled than other single amputees. She was detained for more than two years in various hospitals, emerging in the summer of 1943.

The author spent the first year of his mother's hospitalisation with relations, first on his uncle's farm near Castlewellan in County Down, and then with cousins in the country town of Strabane, County Tyrone. These arrangements proved unsatisfactory and in autumn 1942 his mother tried to place him in a local boarding school. This proved difficult. The Methodist College was full and the only placement on offer was at Cabin Hill, the preparatory school for Campbell College, an establishment

ix

which his mother thought beyond both their means and their way of life. Nevertheless, to Cabin Hill, and subsequently to Campbell College, he went.

I sometimes wonder if it was his education at this exclusive establishment that led eventually to his estrangement from the environment and Christian practices of his boyhood. It is not that I am against education as some of the older generation of my father's contemporaries perhaps were. When I was a young man, I frequently heard an acquaintance of my father remark that there are those who have educated their children to despise them! As an MB, BCh., BAO of the Queen's University, Belfast, I don't think I could be accused of being such a 'backwoodsman' in matters educational. But while I was studying for my Senior Certificate, as it was then called, in sensible, practical subjects like chemistry and biology, my friend, with no father to guide him and left largely to his own devices in a boarding school where his poor mother had little or no influence on his studies, turned towards the 'arts' side of things. It was then that he got a taste for not only the great 'classics' such as Wordsworth and Charles Dickens and William Shakespeare which perhaps do no real harm, but also for 'modern' writers like T. S. Eliot and D. H. Lawrence and James Joyce. From what little I know of these men I believe that they are at worst degenerate and at best a hindrance to any young person who would 'walk with Jesus'. I am sure that it was these and similar authors who made my young friend when he was in his impressionable 'teens' begin to question all the values in which he had been brought up. I would not give houseroom to any work by James Joyce or D. H. Lawrence.

At the end of the Second World War my father got a well-deserved promotion from the insurance company for which he worked, and moved to Belfast as manager of a large district in the south of the city. In consequence, my family once again came to worship in the same assembly of God's people as did the author's mother, who on leaving hospital had taken up residence in that part of Belfast. So although he was for the most of the year at boarding school on the other side of the city in the suburb of Belmont, I was able to renew my friendship with the author during the school holidays and on most Sundays when he travelled home to spend the day with his mother, pushing her in her wheelchair to the various meetings in our gospel hall. I was present on the Lord's Day evening in 1946 when he was baptised, and indeed it was partly under the influence of that experience that I too was baptised and received into the communion of the saints some months later. I praise the Lord that, unlike my old friend, I have now enjoyed the simple fellowship of the Lord's people in the breaking of the bread and the drinking of the wine, in that and in other assemblies, for more than forty years.

It will be clear to the reader of this memoir that the author had begun to stray from 'the old paths' (Jeremiah 6:16) at a very tender age, perhaps even before he was baptised. I believe that we can detect three stages. First, he was afraid to bear witness before rich, godless companions at school and in consequence became a bit ashamed of his fellow believers who came from a much humbler background. Second, he became addicted to worldly pleasures, in particular to the cinema. Third, he began to question from an intellectual point of view the whole basis of our belief, as a result of reading the sort of literature I have already referred to, what his poor mother in later life would often bitterly refer to as 'those old books'.

I had not thought of, still less seen or heard of the author for more than thirty years when, just over a year ago, a very dear friend of mine, well known to the author in his youth, was suddenly called home to be with his Lord. A faithful servant of Christ, he had for many years combined a successful career as chief accountant with one of the great grain merchants in our city with a highly acceptable ministry both to the Lord's people and in the gospel. A short time ago as a relatively young man he decided to 'take early retirement' in order to devote himself 'full-time' to the Lord's work. In less than eighteen months the Lord in His wisdom took him home at the early age of fifty-eight years. His death greatly exercised me, causing me to think of days gone by and of those who once stood with us but no longer did so. Together with my dear wife, I committed the matter to the Lord in prayer. Was it His will that I should seek out my friend and speak to him about eternal matters? It seemed clear to us that we were in the will of the Lord and that very evening I wrote to him.

When we met a few days later we talked about the death of Aaron Bartholomew and I said how impressed one could not help but be by the brevity of life. 'Indeed,' he said, 'we are as grass.' I could not but feel that his tone was flippant but nevertheless I persevered, believing myself to be in the will of the Lord. It was not, he explained, that he took death lightly. Indeed, he thought of death many times every day, and always with horror. Because death, he believed, was the beginning of nothing, the light snuffed out for ever and ever. Last walk, last post, last supper, last nine o'clock news, last day, last hour, last minute and then out over the edge as if we had never been. But why, he wondered, was I so perturbed about Aaron's untimely death? Was I not looking forward to dying?

During the brief time that was left to the author we had quite a number of conversations, for he seemed to welcome my visits. We would frequently talk of the old days, going back more than fifty years. I wish I could say that I was successful in making an impression on him as far as matters spiritual were concerned. On the point that he had raised at our first meeting about the Christian's fear of death, I tried to explain to him that although I had complete confidence in the Resurrection unto everlasting life and that to be absent from the body was to be present with the Lord (2 Corinthians 5:8), nevertheless, while we were in this body the pull of the flesh was very strong, making all of us want to cling to this life. At this he would smile sarcastically. The problem was of course that he knew the arguments as well as I did. However, as those of us who have been redeemed by the precious blood well know, salvation is not a question of knowing an argument, it is a matter of knowing a Person, the Man Christ Jesus.

> I need no other argument,
> I seek no other plea,
> It is enough that Jesus died
> And rose again for me.

On more than one occasion I pressed on him the well-known passage from the Epistle of Paul to the Colossians (2:8): 'Beware lest any man spoil you through philosophy and vain deceit, after the tradition of men, after the rudiments of the world, and not after Christ.' I cannot help wondering if he did not at least sometimes realise that 'the old paths' from which he had so sadly strayed were of greater authority than the 'vain philosophy' and worldly literature on which he had wasted his life. There is, for example, a remarkable passage in these memoirs where the author sets down a dream he had in late life in which he is offered a position by the British Broadcasting Corporation as an introducer of their very popular programme of community hymn-singing, 'Songs of Praise'. In his dream, he sees himself announcing one of the closing hymns, the beautiful and much-loved 'The Day Thou Gavest, Lord, is Ended', to the seaside throng congregated on the sands at Dover. In this dream he is very happy and even writes about the 'sea of faith' coming in. Is it entirely fanciful, I ask myself, to imagine that in this dream he is recalling another seaside scene (the subconscious can play some funny tricks! I speak as a medical man*). I refer to the occasion on Ballyholme beach, Bangor, County Down, just a month before the outbreak of the Second World War, when, under the preaching of a faithful missioner with the CSSM (Children's Special Services Mission), the author, as a little boy just seven years old, first professed faith in the Lord Jesus Christ.

*See S. Freud, *The Interpretation of Dreams.*

To this very day I can remember vividly those meetings and the English evangelist who to our great amusement appeared on the advertisements as Mr Hampshire from Gloucester! On the last evening of the series the 'sea of faith', in the author's striking phrase, was certainly full – full enough to flatten all those sand-castles! Perhaps, after all, that was the 'happy day' that he was to remember, singing about it nearly fifty years later, in a dream–

> O happy day, that fixed my choice
> On Thee my Saviour, and my God!

–the happy day on which a 'great transaction was done' between a seven-year-old boy and his Saviour. If that should be so, it cannot but make one think of the dreadful possibility envisaged by the great apostle himself in his first letter to the Corinthians (9:27) that having preached to others 'I myself should be a castaway'. My friend did just that. He preached to others. How solemn a warning his lost life should be to all young believers.

Along with the manuscript, the author left me a selection of his books, which he said he hoped I would read with profit. Among them are Sir Edmund Gosse's *Father and Son*, frequently referred to in the following pages, and various novels and autobiographies by the Victorian writer Mark Rutherford. In one of these, *The Revolution in Tanner's Lane*, I found tucked away some verses which he had evidently written towards the end of his life. They make sad reading.

ANTHANATOLOGY

Nothing will come of nothing. Think again
On Fleming's trek or Isherwood's ascent,
Where shallow draughts intoxicate the brain,
And our delight is had without content.

From morn to dewy eve, a summer's day,
Indifferent to a beautiful physique,

I see, with hollow eye and wrinkled brow,
Unresting death a whole day nearer now,
The sick man's passport in his hollow beak.
The lone and level sands stretch far away.

As killing as the canker to the rose,
An air that kills from yon far country blows,
And I have that within which passeth show
By storied urn or animated bust.
My words fly up, my thoughts remain below,
Whereof I cannot speak, thereof I must.

The curfew tolls: westward the hot sun lowers,
And each slow dusk a drawing-down of blinds.
Good things of day begin to droop and drowse,
Which by and by black night will take away.
Then comes still evening on and twilight grey,
Shades of the prison house begin to close.
To be imprisoned in the viewless winds!
The winds that will be howling at all hours!

To lie in cold obstruction and to rot
In absence, darkness, death, things which are not!

So do my minutes hasten to their end,
While millions of strange shadows on me tend,
Whereby the horn of plenty is undone.
I saw eternity the other night,
A chamber deaf to noise and blind to light,
And thought of London, spread out in the sun.

I could not but think: What a bleak vision of a Christless eternity!
How sad the unbeliever's prospect of the far country 'from

whose bourn no traveller returns'! Oh, if only the author could have been granted the 'blessed assurance' that death is indeed the sick man's passport – to 'a better world that's waiting in the sky'!

My passport to the realms of bliss
Is 'Jesus died for me'.

Brazilian Adventure and *News from Tartary* by Peter Fleming (1907–71) and *The Ascent of F6* by Christopher Isherwood (1904–86) and W. H. Auden (1907–73) were typical of the books which had such an insidious influence on the author when he was a young man. Here at least he seems to have had 'second thoughts' about this sort of literature and to acknowledge that while it may for a time be 'intoxicating', deep down it is 'shallow' and can provide no lasting contentment.

I tried the broken cisterns Lord
But Ah the waters failed!
Even as I stooped to drink they fled,
And mocked me as I wailed.

The line 'Unresting death a whole day nearer now' is taken from 'Aubade' by Philip Larkin, CH, CBE, a poem which describes very vividly the sort of fear which the author had of death. 'The curfew tolls' is taken from 'The curfew tolls the knell of parting day' which is the opening line of Thomas Gray's famous and much-loved 'Elegy in a Country Churchyard'.

The Autobiography of Mark Rutherford, which, in conversation with me, the author would often refer to as one of his favourite books, has an introduction written by Rutherford's friend Reuben Shapcott. I feel I could not do better than to end my own introductory sketch by quoting some words written by Shapcott about Rutherford, since they are such an apt description of my own poor friend.

It is all very well for remarkable persons to occupy themselves with exalted subjects, which are out of the ordinary road which ordinary humanity treads; but we who are not remarkable make a very great mistake if we have anything to do with them ... Many a man goes into his study, shuts himself up with his poetry or his psychology, comes out, half understanding what he has read, is miserable because he cannot find anybody with whom he can talk about it, and misses the far more genuine joy which he could have had from a game with his children, or listening to what his wife had to tell him about the neighbours ... Metaphysics, including all speculations as to the why and wherefore, are not only for the most part loss of time but are frequently ruinous ... Rutherford was an example of the danger and folly of cultivating thoughts and reading books to which he was not equal, and which tend to make a man lonely.

There are not many joys to compare with the discovery of the right book at the right time. For me, such a book was Edmund Gosse's *Father and Son*, which I read at a gulp one September afternoon when I was seventeen years old. Gosse published his classic in 1907, and, in the preface written in that year, he describes his narrative as 'a *document*, a record of educational and religious conditions which, having passed away, will never return ... the diagnosis of a dying Puritanism'. Gosse was referring to the years of his own childhood and adolescence, the 1850s and 1860s, yet just four pages into his story I recognised the spirit, perfectly caught, of my own early days with the brethren, eighty years later, in the 1930s and 1940s. The religious conditions to which Gosse alludes, the dying Puritanism which he diagnoses, seemed to me to be the conditions which governed my own childhood, when, like Edmund Gosse, I too was the only child of a father and mother who

> found themselves shut outside all Protestant communions, [meeting] only with a few extreme Calvinists like themselves, on terms of what almost may be called negation – with no priest, no rituals, no festivals, no ornament of any kind, nothing but the Lord's Supper and the exposition of the Holy Scriptures drawing these austere souls into any sort of cohesion. They called themselves 'the Brethren' simply; a title enlarged by the world outside into 'Plymouth Brethren'.

Just so. When I was five years old I knew all about the distinction between the Brethren and the Plymouth Brethren. We were not

Plymouth Brethren, my father insisted. After all, as he would explain to me, how could we be Plymouth Brethren when we didn't live in Plymouth? We lived in Bangor, County Down. So we might perhaps be described as Bangor Brethren. But really we were just brethren. And so, on my first day at the local public elementary school, I knew that when I was asked my religion I should advertise myself as brethren *tout court*. What was that? wondered the young teacher who was filling in the register. The Headmaster advised him simply to write OD. What was that? 'Other Denominations,' replied the Head. I imagine that even then, young as I was, I knew that I ought to have entered a protest at this point but that being of a timorous disposition I was afraid to do so. For the truth of the matter was that we were not a denomination at all. My parents would, I imagine, have deprecated Gosse's upper-case Brethren with its denominational ring, which seemed to place us, by what Professor Ryle was some years later to call a category mistake, in company that we did not want to keep: as if there were Baptists and Presbyterians and Methodists and Episcopalians and Brethren – OD, perhaps, but a denomination nevertheless. When the author of the Epistle to the Hebrews wrote (2:11) that Jesus, having sanctified us, was for that cause not ashamed to call us brethren, he did not mean Brethren. Not, I hasten to add, that we would ever have presumed on the relationship by treating it as symmetrical. On the promenade, the Salvation Army with their uncertain grasp of protocol might be heard to sing:

Jesus, our brother, shepherd, friend,
Our prophet, priest and king.

But to the brethren that would have been impertinence. We preferred:

Jesus our *master*, shepherd, friend.

I would have been familiar too with the charge that the

2

unwanted sobriquet was, along with much else, the world's doing. The things the world said about us! It said we were clannish, money-minded, narrow and holier-than-thou, and, as we often reminded ourselves, the world thought that we were peculiar people. 'Those Plymouth Brethren,' said the world, 'those Plyms are very peculiar.' This particular charge was indeed put to good account by the brethren during their impromptu sermons, the world having on this occasion inadvertently got it right, since, according to the Epistle of Paul to Titus (2:14) Christ had redeemed us in order to purify unto himself a peculiar people, zealous of good works. And so the rigmarole would be trotted out, the speaker as pleased with himself as if it had been newly minted: 'The world says those brethren are very peculiar people. Well, beloved brethren, we *are*, God be praised, through Christ's redeeming work, a peculiar people. Holy Scripture itself *says* we are.' By the more learned the words were spoken with a smile, acknowledging some equivocation, but by others more seriously.

Intramurally, the brethren would refer to themselves, without the least self-consciousness, as saints. They did this on the grounds that it was ordinary New Testament usage so to refer to all believers. Accordingly when a brother moved house, or even when he went on holiday, he would carry with him a letter of commendation, obligatory in our strict circle and known simply as a 'letter' – 'Have you got your letter?' – which would read something like this:

> From the saints who meet at the Knightsbridge Gospel Hall, Sunshine Street, Belfast, to the saints who meet at Stoke-on-Trent, England – Greetings, in the Name of the Lord Jesus Christ! We commend to your loving care and Christian fellowship our brother Mr Bleaney who will be on his holidays in your district. Receive him in the Lord, as becometh saints. On behalf of the above assembly, Yours in His service [*or*, Yours in heavenly bonds, *or*, Yours till He come, *or*, Yours because His], Moses Bartholomew and Gibson Stevenson.

3

Even though Mr Bleaney was well-known to the Stoke saints, having spent his holidays with cousins there for the past twenty years, he would have been thought remiss had he failed on any summer to approach the elders for up-to-date certification of his good standing as a saint. For although we were styled 'open' rather than 'exclusive' brethren, we were not excessively open. Indeed we were rather exclusive compared with some liberal assemblies we had heard of in the south of England who would admit to the breaking of bread any holidaying stranger off the street who professed to be a Christian and sought communion with them, perhaps a Baptist or even a Presbyterian, regardless of whether or not he had a letter indicating that he had been baptised and received into the fellowship of a *bona fide* assembly of 'open' brethren. Verse 15 of Psalm 116 was a popular ingredient in brethren death notices. 'Precious in the sight of the Lord is the death of his saints.'

There was nothing special about saints, as the world and especially the Roman Catholic Church (so-called) would try to insinuate, a saint being nothing more (and, importantly, nothing less) than a sinner saved by grace. Sainthood was not in the gift of the Pope, and of his canonisations, his Joans, his Anselms, his Bernadettes, his Malachys and his Sebastians we knew little and would have preferred to know less. Since they had in all likelihood never been born again they were very probably not even saints, never mind Saints. We were reluctant to refer even to Paul, Peter, Matthew, James and the rest as saints since although they were of course saints they were saints no more (and no less) than was Mr Bleaney. To refer to *Saint* Matthew was to fall into the worldly trap of seeming to mark a distinction where there was none. When just beginning to preach, I would, in order to fill up the time, slowly and pompously request the congregation to open their bibles at the Second Epistle of *Saint* Paul to the Thessalonians, relishing every word. I was rebuked. To us he was plain Paul, or, if we wanted to emphasise his special status

4

as a soul-winner and minister, 'Paul the great apostle to the Gentiles', or, deferring to the typically vain hyperbole of his First Epistle to Timothy, 'Paul the chief of sinners'. These nice points of doctrine were as familiar to me in 1940 as they would have been to the young Edmund Gosse eighty years earlier.

Why then was Gosse so confident in 1907 that he was producing a document which was already, in an age when all was changed utterly, of merely historical interest? Had he become so grand in his friendships with Hardy and Beerbohm, with Henry James and Arthur Balfour, with Haldane and the Londonderrys, that the unsophisticated lives and practices which he was describing now seemed impossibly remote? Did the great metropolitan critic never go back to Devon or even, out of sentimental curiosity, seek out the gospel halls of Clapham or Blackheath or Hackney or Wembley or Deptford or Burnt Oak, which must have been thriving then, since they assuredly were forty years later? Or did he mean that the way of life he was writing about was gone for ever as far as educated persons were concerned. That can hardly be the case since in the milieu he describes, his father, a Fellow of the Royal Society, was so exceptional as to be accepted as a sort of pastor to the assembly of simple folk in which he ministered, a recognition which would not have been so readily forthcoming amongst the brethren of my youth who with their strong insistence on the priesthood of *all* believers would recognise no *primus inter pares*. Since, even in Gosse's youth, the brethren were by and large far from sophisticated, they surely could not be said to have passed into history merely through the loss of their better-educated members.

Indeed, I imagine that in both Gosse's youth and middle age, as in my own youth, the brethren rather gloried in their general inferiority as evidence that they were in the right place. For had not Paul himself written that not many wise men after the flesh, not many mighty, not many noble are called, God having chosen the foolish things of the world to confound the wise, and the

5

weak to confound the things that are mighty (1 Corinthians 1:26–7)? This complacent humility was not incompatible with an attitude of respect, even of deference, towards those of the more talented, mightier, nobler or merely better-off minority who had succeeded against the odds in getting themselves called too. A certain Lady Huntingdon ('of Lady Huntingdon's Connection', the brethren never failed to add, somehow making her sound even grander) was frequently quoted as having remarked that she thanked God for the little letter *m* in that the great apostle had not written: not *any* mighty, not *any* noble are called. This *mot* was much appreciated by the brethren and not to the smallest degree resented as being somewhat *de haut en bas*.

Besides, there is educated and educated, and while I never knew an FRS amongst the brethren, there were in my time medical doctors galore, a Professor of Greek, a member of His Majesty's Inspectorate of Schools, a future director-general of the National Economic and Development Council and at least one Permanent Secretary of a civil service department (albeit in the corridors of Stormont rather than those of Whitehall): all what my parents would have called 'thousand-a-year men', and respected rather than envied for it. These educated ones were remarkable for the nice sense of *enjambement* with which they would give out, that is, announce or propose a hymn.

Take my life and let it be consecrated,
Lord, to Thee.

This would be their version, rather than as the rude mechanicals, the riveters, the bus inspectors, the bread deliverymen and the chargehands would have it:

Take my life and let it be,
Consecrated Lord to Thee.

What I, as a backslidden, i.e., lapsed, seventeen-year-old brother felt the lack of in my brethren background was not educated

6

persons but intellectuals or, better, men of letters. I did not mean of course intellectuals or men of letters among actually practising brethren since I would at that age have been sufficiently arrogant to think 'intelligent Christian', to say nothing of 'intellectual brother', a contradiction in terms, but rather men of letters with a brethren background, fellow apostates who had actually been through it, survived and then written it down. The James Joyce of *A Portrait of the Artist as a Young Man* or, even better, the Joyce of *Stephen Hero* was all very well in his way, but the Roman Catholic way was something very far removed from our way. I had no idea that such a writer and such a book existed, an acknowledged masterpiece to boot, praised by Kipling as more interesting than *David Copperfield*, until that chance opening of *Father and Son*. It was a Cortezian moment.

Like Gosse I was the only child of a parent widowed when I was very young. Where he had a father, I had a mother. My mother's parents, unlike my father's, were first-generation brethren, my maternal grandfather having discovered as a pious, God-fearing, hymn-singing young Presbyterian farmer that churchgoing and clean living would not keep him out of hell and that he needed, as the brethren unembarrassedly expressed it, to be saved. He in turn converted, as the world might have put it (led her to Christ, we would have said), my grandmother Margaret Murdoch, great-aunt of the distinguished novelist, much to the indignation of her superior family. I have no memories of these grandparents, as they died some years before I was born, but my grandfather's bearded, somewhat lugubrious face stares out at me from the cover of a gospel tract widely distributed when I was young.

THOMAS R. MAXWELL OF CARRYDUFF

The subject of this tract was a County Down farmer Thomas R. Maxwell, of Ashvale House, Carryduff. He was brought up

7

religiously and was a regular attender at the local Presbyterian Meeting-house, and also a member of the choir.

Well nigh sixty years ago Mr Thomas Lough and Dr Matthews pitched a tent in that district. As these faithful men preached nightly, stressing the absolute necessity of being born again (John 3:7) the Holy Ghost began to deal with him, and deep conviction was wrought within his heart. The dread realities of eternity gripped his soul and he could sing truthfully McCheyne's words:

> When free grace awoke me
> By light from on high,
> Then legal fears shook me,
> I trembled to die.

On August 5th, 1880, when working in the fields, he was led to trust in Christ through Romans chapter 4, verse 25, 'Who was delivered for our offences, and was raised again for our justification.' For the first time in his life he saw the great truth of substitution – that God's beloved Son upon the cross had been delivered for his offences and raised again for his justification. Realising that a Holy God had punished His Son, the guiltless One, for him the guilty one, he believed the good news and became the happy possessor of everlasting life (John 3:16). For almost fifty years he lived in the enjoyment of peace with God (Romans 5:1) passing into the presence of the Lord on 11th December, 1928. Throughout those years, in halls, in the open-air, and in personal conversation, he sought to warn men and women of coming judgment and of the necessity of the New Birth. As the hymn writer has put it:

> How solemn are the words
> And yet to faith how plain,
> Which Jesus uttered while on earth,
> Ye must be born again.

The tract is signed A.A.R. and I found recently among some old papers an acrostic over the same initials in which A.A.R. is not

8

far short of fulsome in praise of his old friend, in the brethren manner always ready to supply chapter and verse.

T	here was a man of high degree,	Acts 13:22
H	eavenly minded all could see,	Colossians 3:1
O	verseeing God's little flock,	Acts 20:28
M	aking much of Christ the rock.	Matthew 16:18
A	man that walked in separation,	Psalms 1:1
S	aved and enjoying God's salvation,	Deuteronomy 33:29
R	ejoicing and glad in the new creation.	2 Corinthians 5:17
M	any a weary mile he trod,	John 4:6
A	ssured like Enoch pleasing God,	Hebrews 11:4
X	alting Christ to saint and sinner,	Colossians 1:28
W	atering the old and the young beginner,	1 John 2:13
E	ver defending doctrine sound,	Titus 1:9
L	etting his light shine all around	Philippians 2:15
L	ifted up home awaiting his crown.	2 Timothy 4:6–8

My father was of similar stock, from Ballywillwill, near Annsborough in County Down, where his father was a rather more substantial farmer than Mr Maxwell. This grandfather was not a convert, but from a family long 'amongst brethren', as we would put it, in order to avoid the dreaded denominational implication. We did not go to or belong to the Brethren, still less the Plymouth Brethren – we were amongst brethren. My widowed mother would tell me in later years that I was, on my father's side, seventh-generation brethren. This, if true, which seems to me unlikely, would mean that one of my ancestors was perhaps a founding father of the movement. My paternal grandfather, however, his orthodox background notwithstanding, was never to my knowledge the hero of a gospel tract, perhaps because in the pursuit of substance, pulling down his barns and building greater, he had not trodden so many weary miles 'xalting Christ. Nevertheless, Robert Wright of Ballywillwill would have been in complete agreement with Thomas Maxwell of Carryduff as to the nature of God's salvation, separation from the world and sound doctrine, as would my father and mother after them. And Philip Gosse FRS would have found entirely congenial all they believed in, from a historical Garden of Eden and a factual record of the doings of the patriarchs, the judges and the kings of Israel, to the death, burial and resurrection of Jesus Christ, His second coming, the tribulation, the last judgment at the great white throne and a subsequent eternity to be spent either in heaven with Christ or, with the Christ-rejecters, in a lake of fire burning with brimstone, where there will be weeping and wailing and gnashing of teeth and their worm dieth not and their fire is not quenched. On all this they would have agreed down to the finest detail (the brethren are strong on minutiae). For example, will the Church be 'raptured' before or after the great tribulation? Answer: before.

On the subject of the Garden of Eden it must be admitted that Gosse was a bit of an original, somewhat more adventurous than any of the brethren I knew. In 1857, as a fundamentalist who was also the associate of Darwin, Wallace, Hooker and Lyell, Philip Gosse felt under a very special constraint to declare himself on the apparently growing tension between science and revealed religion in the matter of the biblical account of the Creation. What could he say? He could not for one moment deny Archbishop Ussher's calculation from the patriarchal genealogies that the universe was created at 6 p.m. on Sunday, 23 October, in the year 4004 BC, but he could attempt to reconcile that undoubted truth with the apparent geological evidence that had persuaded his contemporaries in the Royal Society that the earth was much older. Fifty years later the son was to write:

> Geology certainly *seemed* to be true, but the Bible, which was God's word, *was* true. If the Bible said that all things in Heaven and Earth were created in six days, created in six days they were – in six literal days of twenty-four hours each.

10

So, as readers of *Father and Son* will remember, Gosse proposed that just as God had certainly created a garden complete with lions with well-developed molars, to say nothing of mature cedars of Lebanon that were to all appearances many years and not mere days old, so he had created an earth whose apparent fossil age was not its real age. In this way Gosse confidently resolved the chicken–egg conundrum in favour of the chicken. After all, as the great naturalist famously speculated, Adam and Eve would each have had an omphalos, which might insinuate the *suggestio falsi* that they had been born, rather than sculpted out of dust and cartilage respectively. My brethren, however, did not take Darwin and the geologists beneath their notice, beyond pitying those unfortunate, deluded people who could bring themselves to believe that they were descended from monkeys, and they would surely have thought speculation about Adam's navel rude.

When I was nine years old my father was killed. On the night of 15 April 1941 there was a heavy air raid on Belfast. We lived twelve miles away in Bangor, then a middling-sized seaside resort. One bomber, lightening his load for the long haul home, dropped his last bomb in our front garden. And so as I fled the house where my mother lay, or so it has always seemed to me in what must surely be a nightmare quasi-memory, at some distance from one of her legs, I saw my father for the last time, dying at the turn of the stairs.

My memories of my father are jejune, suggesting to me that I must have suppressed a good deal, perhaps out of an early reluctance to be drawn into a sentimental communion with my grieving mother. 'Do you remember when your father ...?' she must often have asked, and I imagine that my response was frequently ungracious and negative. I do remember that he bought me a secondhand bicycle and had the good sense to push me vigorously down the incline which led from Broadway into Hazeldene Gardens, so that after only two tumbles I was up and away, as free as Marie in the mountains. He bought a secondhand baby Austin which even then looked out of date, and then delighted me by buying another which, though still secondhand, was the very latest edition. One dark night at the beginning of the Second World War, between Newtownards and Conlig, we ran out of petrol. My father went to the nearest farmhouse and returned with a can of what he claimed was airforce petrol which, strictly speaking, he said, we should not be using. For the remaining miles I entertained the liveliest expectation that we would take off, if only a foot or so above the tarmacadam.

The few memories I have of my father are for the most part centred on the brethren and their gospel hall in Central Avenue, Bangor, which were such a large part of his life and therefore, perforce, of mine. Of this assembly he was, though comparatively young, an elder, or in our jargon one of the overseeing brethren, or, for short, one of the oversight. I was proud of him as in this capacity he led the open-air meetings on blustery summer evenings before the war in the extravagantly named Marine Gardens under the McKee Clock.

> Then let our songs abound
> And every tear be dry.
> We're marching through Immanuel's ground
> To fairer worlds on high.
> We're marching to Zion,
> Beautiful, beautiful Zion,
> We're marching upward to Zion,
> The beautiful city of God.

The world strolled past sucking icecream sliders (wafers) and pokes (as cones or cornets were innocently styled by our cold maids) totally indifferent to the beautiful city of God. This was only to be expected for as the world would shortly learn, perhaps from my father, wide is the gate, and broad is the way that leadeth to destruction, and *many* there be which go in thereat, while strait is the gate and narrow is the way which leadeth unto life, and *few* there be that find it (Matthew 7:13–14). Certainly the summer crowds appeared to confirm Matthew in his pessimistic estimates, and in memory our group seems pathetically small, perhaps surprisingly so when you remember that this was the evangelical, Protestant northeast of Ireland in the unpermissive 1930s.

One curious memory is of my father's frequent ministry to the assembled saints at the Lord's Day morning meeting. On these occasions he was often moved to read from the Book of Psalms and invariably that odd little word 'Selah' would be pronounced by him not once but several times. As, for example, 'Hear my prayer, O God; give ear to the words of my mouth. For strangers are risen up against me, and oppressors seek after my soul: they have not set God before them. Selah' (Psalm 54:3). Or, a firm favourite: 'When I kept silence, my bones waxed old through my roaring all the day long. For day and night thy hand was heavy upon me: my moisture is turned into the drought of summer. Selah' (Psalm 32:3–4). I was always very impressed by the authority, not to say the insouciance, with which my father delivered himself of this mysterious vocable, just as if he knew what it meant. Did he know what it meant? Did I ever ask him? If so, I have forgotten.

On one occasion I found myself covered with reflected glory through the visit of my father's first cousin, who was to stay with us while conducting a week of special meetings in the gospel hall. This cousin was a celebrated missionary, and was known throughout our little community, in the style of famous evangelical missionaries of the past like Fred Stanley Arnott of Africa and Hudson Taylor of China, as Bobbie Wright of Japan. He was home on his first leave, or 'furlough', as the missionaries would refer to it, savouring the military nuance. On his first Sunday he 'took' the Sunday school and we heard from the horse's mouth about the rather dim prospects of those unfortunate children who had been foolish enough to be born in heathen darkness and about whom it was our custom to sing on most Sunday afternoons.

When mothers of Salem their children brought to Jesus,
The stern disciples drove them back and bade them depart.
But Jesus saw them ere they fled
And sweetly looked and kindly said,
'Suffer the children to come unto Me.'

14

How kind was the Saviour to bid those children welcome,
But there are many thousands who have never heard His Name.
The Bible they have never read,
They know not that the Saviour said,
'Suffer the children to come unto Me.'

Then Bobbie taught us to sing 'Jesus Loves Me' in Japanese
('Wah Gah Shoo Yessu' or phonemes roughly to that effect). But
this was kid's stuff. At the evening meetings, which I was given
a special, late-to-bed dispensation to attend, the grown-ups were
encouraged to sing, to the splendid rollicking tune of 'Bringing
in the Sheaves':

Bringing Japanese, bringing Japanese,
We shall come rejoicing, bringing Japanese.

Six years old, I blushed with embarrassed pleasure, anticipating
that golden harvest evening when we would carry in from the
fields great yellow stooks of saved Japanese sinners to lay at the
Saviour's feet.

Within the year, Bobbie had returned to Japan where he was
caught by the war and languished in Japanese internment camps.
He survived to return (like General MacArthur) for a post-
bellum tour of duty. In later life he would describe, affectingly (I
suppose), his joy at being met on the quay at Yokohama by eight
Japanese brethren who had kept the faith, through trials and
tribulations both psychological and physical that had forced
others into apostasy. Doubtless it is only the world, with its
miscalculated priorities, that would think the cost of bringing
the good news from Tyrone to Tokyo a bit excessive. At the time,
of course, I found it entirely natural that Bobbie should have
obeyed the injunction to go into all the world and preach the
gospel to every creature (Mark 16:15), devoting his life to bringing a handful of Japanese ('where two or three are gathered
together in my name, there am I in the midst of them' – Matthew
18:20) into little assemblies of born-again Christians just like

those in which he himself had grown up in Omagh and Letterkenny and Fintona and Castlederg, in his home town of Strabane, and five miles down the road at Sion Mills, locus of the story of the doubtless apocryphal brethren death notice, the encomium of which was transmitted to the newspaper as 'For forty years a watcher on Sion's hills' only to appear as 'For forty years a watchman at Sion Mills'.

In the monthly newsletters with which Bobbie kept the saints 'at home' up to date with his activities, we get a glimpse of the bizarre enterprise to which this serious but not solemn (or perhaps solemn but not serious) young man had committed himself.

> [29 April 1933] I plod on, sometimes bemoaning my own barrenness, at other times, topping a crest and getting a glimpse of the glory-land and the One and Welcome awaiting me there, so I hitch up my kit and add another inch to my stride. Well, we'll soon be there, the last skirmish over, the last mile-stone past, then Home and Rest forever.

At the time of writing the valetudinarian would have been just twenty-seven years old.

Then, there is a joke, or perhaps a 'joke'. 'We had another "funeral" yesterday. The wife of one baptised in January was herself baptised.'

> [16 March 1936] The children's meeting each night gives us joy. They can sing the names of the books of the Bible, the ten commandments and a number of hymns from memory; but it is souls, souls we want. Do you realize that the way to the Cross is much longer in Japan? The belief in the hundreds of local deities has to be replaced by faith in the One True God; and acceptance of the Bible as the superhuman and unerring Word of God, and knowledge of sin outside of lawbreaking have all to occur before they are on the same ground as the sinner at home.

So much ground to be made up before the Japanese sinner was

on level terms with a decent, godless monotheist from Sion Mills, who at least acknowledged that the Bible was the Good Book and who had a properly developed sense of sin. In the meantime, taking their first step in the right direction, the Japanese children sing, 'Genesis, Exodus, Leviticus, Numbers, Deuteronomy, Joshua, Judges, Ruth … '

[4 May 1936] The Sanatorium work gives results, but in a few months these have 'gone home'. We long to see lives as well as souls saved. Recently Fuji-moto San was led to visit a home a day earlier than usual and found a mother who had written farewell letters and was about to commit suicide. Pray for her soul's salvation.

[14 July 1936] The 'would-be' suicide of the previous 'Tidings' got saved and has since died. 'Only a few week's difference,' you will say. Yes, but what a difference! Instead of the flames of an eternal hell licking her Christless soul, she is in Heaven today, welcomed there by a nail-pierced hand. Would you ask me to exchange thrills like this for the old thrills of Sales Records, Salary Advances, etc.?

Did he truly believe it, that if he had not, in 1931, in obedience to the Lord's call, taken himself off to Japan, a dying woman would have committed suicide in a sanatorium and would now be in hell, her Christless soul licked by the eternal flames? If he did, then surely we can say with some confidence what Gosse said in 1907, that his story is part of a 'record of educational and religious conditions which, having passed away, will never return'? He did believe it, but I doubt that we can with any confidence claim that much has changed.

Certainly when more than fifty years after the diary entries I have just quoted I attended Bobbie's funeral in a small gospel hall in Whitehead, County Antrim, not a great deal seemed to have changed. We sang his favourite hymn:

17

Yes, He's a friend of mine
And He with me does all things share.
Since all is Christ's, and Christ is mine,
Why should I have a care?
For Jesus is a friend of mine.

Then the missionary's work was gratefully recalled by his several memorialists, mention being made of all those Japanese believers who would never even have heard of Jesus Christ had not Bobbie obeyed the call, but whom he was now, it was alleged, at this very moment, joyfully re-encountering face to face (*face to face*?) in heaven. But what of the future? worried the preacher.

Far, far away, in heathen darkness dwelling,
Millions of souls forever may be lost.
Who, who will go, salvation's story telling?
Looking to Jesus, counting not the cost?

What Elisha would inherit Bobbie's mantle? In one of his 1936 newsletters he had written: 'Over five millions have passed off this scene unwarned into a lost eternity and a new population of ten millions have replaced them since I left Ireland, YET not one has felt constrained by the love of Christ to come and help.' The burden of all those millions and now, as we were reminded, in the age of Nissan and Sony and Honda and the Nikkei Dow Index, untold millions upon millions more, should weigh heavily upon us, all of them likely, nay certain to be lost for ever, unless young brethren from County Antrim should respond to the call. 'For how shall they hear without a preacher?' (Romans 10:14). Where, oh where, implored the speaker, were the young men who would follow the departed warrior?

How sweet 'twould be at evening,
If you and I could say
Good Shepherd we've been seeking
The sheep that went astray.

18

Oh! Who will go and find them?
In the paths of death they roam.
At the close of the day 'twill be sweet to say
I have brought some lost one home.

Although I was not present when Bobbie set out on his travels, I can well believe that there was some preacher on hand at his 'farewell meeting' to give the required readings from verses 37–8 of chapter 9 of the Gospel According to Matthew. 'The harvest truly is plenteous, but the labourers are few; Pray ye therefore the Lord of the harvest, that he will send forth labourers into his harvest', and from verse 35 of chapter 4 of John's Gospel, 'Say not ye, There are yet four months and *then* cometh harvest? behold, I say unto you, Lift up your eyes and look on the fields; for they are white already to harvest.' And so it was, nearly sixty years later, at the end. Look on the fields, implores the preacher, and the inevitable question is put: if the harvest fields were white in 1931, how much whiter must they now be in 1988?

As an adolescent, little inclined to be sceptical, Gosse nevertheless 'thought it impossible that a secret of such stupendous importance should have been entrusted to a little group of Plymouth Brethren, and have been hidden from millions of disinterested and pious theologians'. For it was not only the Japanese and Chinese who were in ignorance, needing to be saved through the atoning death of Jesus Christ and then baptised and gathered into little meetings run on what we called 'assembly lines', but the great mass of Christendom had, to varying degrees, got it wrong too. The brethren, in their unpastored, unornamented assemblies were the only group to score a bull's eye with respect to God's purposes for mankind. While I was still very young I could have positioned all the sects on the target board according to how they approximated to the ideal. Thus the Baptists scored an inner (because they appreciated the scriptural truth of baptism by immersion), the Methodists a magpie for John Wesley's sake (it was many years before Lord Soper), Presbyterians and evangelical Episcopalians an outer. Satanically inspired deviants, like Jehovah's Witnesses, Christian Scientists, Seventh Day Adventists and the Church of Jesus Christ of the Latter Day Saints were not on the board at all.

Roman Catholics, *en masse*, were also excluded though my mother would probably have agreed with Gosse *père* 'that here and there a pious and extremely ignorant individual, who had not comprehended the errors of the Papacy, but had humbly studied his Bible, could hope to find eternal life'. Following her

20

amputation, some Limerick nuns who had heard her sad story sent my mother a small plaque which took the form of a cushion on which they had picked out in coloured beads the name JESUS. This vulgar gew-gaw she hung in a prominent place. Aesthetically, I dare say it was no worse than the Sunday school prizes which decorated the walls of brethren bedrooms, washed-out prints of Highland cattle knee-deep in Scotland ('I will fear no evil', Psalm 23:4), or a bearded Middle Eastern shepherd with his mountainy flock ('I am the good shepherd, and know my sheep', John 10:14), or Edinburgh Castle ('God is our refuge and strength', Psalm 46:1) the text in fancy lettering against a sepia sky, though never to my knowledge, and the ribald world notwithstanding, 'Behold, I come quickly' (Revelation 3:11) over the bedhead.

The plaque/cushion did, or so it seemed to me, contribute its own characteristically papist nuance to the vulgarity, not quite on the level of an exposed and bleeding heart or of the pale Galilean with the nimbus, but distinctly unbrethren for all that. Nevertheless, these Limerick nuns, having spared a thought for my mother in her time of affliction, were ever after acknowledged by her as Christians, however cruelly misguided. She never failed to remember them in her prayers, conceiving of them, I imagine, as sisters *manquées*, poor souls who would have liked nothing better than to leap over the wall of their convent and join the Limerick saints in simple New Testament assembly fellowship amongst brethren, had they not been cruelly incarcerated by their wicked priests.

Late in her life my mother told me that she would dearly have liked to have heard Mr Billy Graham preach, and on one occasion had been sorely tempted to go to one of his meetings. She had not gone because it would have been wrong to do so, since he did not appreciate the truths of assembly fellowship and was in consequence one from whom we were enjoined by the apostle Paul to come out and be separate (2 Corinthians 6:17). Because of the importance they placed on the distinction between a bull's eye

21

and an inner, the brethren surely suffered the oddest temptations.

Mr Graham was saved – probably. The same could not be said of many of the clergy or even of all those who styled themselves evangelical. When I was a young believer, one of the stars among the numerous brethren preachers who were, as we put it, full-time in the Lord's work, having resigned what they called their secular employment to live on whatever offerings the Holy Spirit moved the saints to send them, was a Mr Harold Paisley, the elder brother of Ian whose world notoriety was as yet many years off, but who was already beginning to make a local name for himself as a firebrand and Free Presbyterian scourge of the orthodox Presbyterians. On the whole we were in favour of this, since as was well known, the Presbyterians were at best Laodicean, and at worst riddled with modernism. However, Ian Paisley *did* wear his collar back to front and he *did* style himself *Reverend*. Apropos of that usage, we were much given to quoting, with a knowing look, from Psalm 111, verse 9, 'Holy and reverend is his name'. We would then go on to remark with a self-satisfied smirk that the Pope having stolen one of God's names, the clergymen had stolen the other.

So Ian Paisley, while an object of some interest to the brethren, could not be said to be without reservation a good thing. Accordingly, when Harold came to tea my mother sought his opinion of his younger brother. Now Harold had high standards. He had been known to preach against young brethren who on their holidays wore sports jackets with a vent at the back and against young preachers who raised their arms to God in supplication for the purpose, he alleged, of revealing to the congregation an expensive wristwatch with an *expanding gold strap*. Such display was of the flesh and the elder Mr Paisley taught a generation of young evangelists that when they went preaching they should put their watches in their pockets. So it was not perhaps surprising that the great preacher should opine, 'I sometimes wonder if Ian is saved at all.'

22

Forty years on the doubt persists. J. L. Austin has alleged that in philosophy 'actually, "really" is like "actually", really a broken reed'. That will certainly be the case too in theology. Did Christ *really* feed a multitude with five small loaves and two fishes? Did He *really* rise from the dead on the third day? It will all depend on what we mean by 'feed' and 'rise from the dead' and to the better sort of theologian I am sure these questions must seem naive. Nevertheless, I cannot help wondering (in 1990) if Mr Paisley is *really* a saint. Does he *really* (and truly) love the Lord Jesus with all his heart and trust Him as his own and personal saviour?

'No priest, no ritual, no festivals, no ornaments of any kind', writes Gosse. One ornament rejected by most brethren, at least in my time, was any artificial or instrumental aid to hymn singing. No piano, organ or harmonium graced or disgraced their gospel halls. There were, admittedly, two or three exceptions, for example at the small seaside resort of Ballywalter, in the Holborn Hall in Bangor, and in central Belfast, where the Victoria Hall aimed, without much success as the world would have judged the matter, for a fashionable congregation. But these assemblies, because of their organ-owning and other related activities such as bright Saturday evening get-togethers for young believers (The Help-Heavenward! The Rendezvous!) where the singing of solos and duets (the Bennett Sisters) was not unheard of, were considered 'loose' (our word for relaxed) in contrast to the 'tight' (i.e., strict) majority. Moreover, even these loose assemblies on the Lord's Day or the first day of the week (never 'on Sunday' and never, that errant Presbyterianism, 'the Sabbath') employed an organist only for the evening, or gospel meeting, when it could be argued a musical accompaniment encouraged the cheery or at least tuneful singing which might encourage the ungodly (our friends, in the preacher's euphemism) to come in off the street and hear words whereby they might be saved. In the Lord's Day morning, or as it was sometimes called, the worship, or breaking of bread, or remembrance meeting ('This do in remembrance of me') the loose minority concurred with the tight majority

24

in praising the Lord without benefit of man-made instrument.

As in so much of the brethren's practice, what was desired here and, alas, frequently desiderated, was spontaneity, an openness, as they would have put it, to the guidance of the Holy Spirit. Thus, just as there was no formal ordering of procedure in the morning meeting, so that one brother might pray, another might praise, and yet another might simply read, or read and expound the Scripture, as the Lord led, so it must have been felt that in the very singing of the hymns an organist or a piano player would, through his guiding or regulating function, usurp the role of the Spirit.

In principle, if not in practice, any brother (but no sister) might start the singing, leaving the rest of the congregation to follow him as best they might. Certainly nobody was styled, in the Scottish manner, precentor, and indeed, I was of mature years and long since secretly backslidden before I saw in a Glasgow assembly my first real precentor, complete with his accreditation, a large tuning fork which he struck against his elbow to give us the pitch.

Although we would have thought the office, like the equipment, worldly, it must be admitted that the office did exist, albeit forkless, in fact if not in name. In most assemblies some senior brother, not always the most tuneful, would by long custom have acquired the tenancy of which he was jealous. So when some likely young baritone, having given out a hymn, then himself started the singing all in a rush so as to pre-empt the older man, the incumbent was vexed, and the feeling of the meeting was usually with him and against the pretender. In our meeting, there was one such constant offender, a young man called Livingstone Mulholland, thought uppity because, although in humble employment as either a milkman or breadserver, he dressed on Sundays in a black jacket and pinstripe trousers. On one occasion Livingstone not only led the singing but embarked on a tune which, while a familiar enough

25

common-measure tune, was not the accepted tune of the hymn in question. It was 'Lloyd' or 'French' perhaps where one might confidently have expected 'Wiltshire'. I can well understand the young man's thought: it was *his* hymn, was it not, the Holy Spirit having put it into *his* head, and might not ... indeed, had not the same Holy Spirit proposed a change of tune, just this once? However, our quasi-precentor would have nothing of it, saw his opportunity, and after only one verse held up his hand, saying, 'I think we'll have the proper tune, brother,' and resumed his leadership. Livingstone Mulholland had gone too far.

This quasi-precentor's office, which was provocative of so much of the envy and self-advertisement we officially deplored, was called, not as one might have expected, 'leading' or 'starting' the singing, but, more quaintly, 'raising the singing' or 'raising the hymns'. Mr Stevenson, it might be said, raises the hymns in our meeting. Why it should have been so called was never clear to me. It can hardly have been because the description was frequently apt and raise the hymn was just what our leader did, sometimes by nearly an octave, so that after a few bars only the most tremulous sopranos were still in competition. Here was a chance for the aspirant, fraught with danger as is the nature of chances. An incisive, well-pitched, fresh start would be commendable. Clearly in such a case the young man, if he could bring it off, would have some cause to claim that he had been led by the Spirit where the elder had not been. Given a run of three or four successful relaunches the meeting might accept that the Holy Spirit Himself was, if not actually putting down a formal motion in respect of a change in the leadership, at least dropping a heavy hint. However, all too often some principle of overcompensation seemed to operate so that the second attempt was as low of the mark as the first had been high and all but the profoundest basses would be floundering. Since God is not the author of confusion (1 Corinthians 14:33) obviously neither singer could have been led by the Spirit and so both had some

26

cause to feel ashamed.

Prayer books were of course unheard of, or if heard of certainly unresorted to. The brethren were expected to pour out their heart to the Lord in a way that would hardly have been possible had they been reading from a prepared script. In the near-tautology of the General Epistle of James (5:16) it is the effectual *fervent* prayer of the righteous man that availeth much. But our extempore prayers were another source of that confusion which will result when a wilful brother has not submitted himself to the guidance of the Spirit.

Two brethren at opposite ends of the hall would rise simultaneously to pray. Each would begin with a low, slow growl, which would gradually intensify both in pitch and in pace. Brow furrowed, eyes tightly shut in concentration, evidence, as they might, and often did say, that they were, like the patriarch Jacob of old, prepared if need be to wrestle all night with God Almighty (Genesis 32:24), neither would be aware of the other for perhaps as long as fifteen seconds, when one or the other would either hear the opposition or have his coat-tail tugged by his wife and sit down greatly embarrassed. One habitual offender was suspected of carrying on, even while knowing that he was not on his own, thus turning the *contretemps* into a trial of strength with the hoped-for implication that it was the victor who had been in the Spirit all the time, although certainly there is no such implication.

Longwindedness in prayer was with the brethren no vice. On the contrary, there was some competition among the senior brethren as to who would be the most prolix. Spontaneous prayers were, however, difficult to sustain over the longer run, say fifteen minutes and upwards. Here hymns played a useful auxiliary part, extensive quotation therefrom padding out the prayer. Thus a brother might advert in his prayer to 'the hymn-writer' who had 'put it so beautifully' when he wrote, 'How sweet the name of Jesus sounds in a believer's ear; it soothes his

27

sorrows, heals his wounds and drives away his fear', continuing through half a dozen verses of the familiar hymn while he recovered his more inventive breath. Everyone had his favourites, some of which would crop up on each occasion that the brother felt led to pray. Mr Gibson Stevenson, the insurance agent who raised the hymns and was the competitive prayer who was disinclined to yield the floor, was especially fond of a piece of doggerel to the effect that if the ocean were filled with ink and the sky made of parchment and every blade of grass a quill and every man a professional writer there would not be enough ink or space to write a complete account of God's love. It was part of brethren folklore that these verses had been written by an inmate of a lunatic asylum. Why this alleged fact was thought worthy of remark may not be immediately obvious to the outsider, but I suspect that the moral of the story was that the madman, although deranged, had, through the grace of God, never lost contact with the great truth that no account of the divine love will ever be definitive. And so Mr Stevenson would never fail to slot his favourite into his prayer in a way which must have sounded odd to one hearing him for the first time without the required background knowledge. 'As the lunatic,' he would intone, 'has put to so beautifully':

Could I with ink the ocean fill
And were the sky of parchment made,
Were every blade of grass a quill,
And every man a scribe by trade.
To write the love
Of God above
Would drain the ocean dry,
Nor could the scroll
Contain the whole,
Though stretched from sky to sky.

Why, so many years later, do so many of these mindless ditties complete with their tunes still rattle about my head?

> In spite of myself the insidious mastery of song
> Betrays me back, till the heart of me weeps to belong
> To the old fond evenings at home with winter outside,
> And hymns in the cosy parlour, the tinkling piano our guide.

Asked to rank in order of merit, say, Shelley and jazz and *Lieder* and love and hymn tunes, I would have to say that Shelley and jazz I can take or leave, that *Lieder* and love are fine, but that hymns and hymn tunes have always been something special. Because of exposure to both the brethren hymnology and, at Campbell College, to some sort of public-school hymnal out of *Hymns Ancient and Modern*, my repertoire is both large and eclectic, ranging from

> There is power, power, wonder-working power
> In the precious blood of the Lamb

sung to the tune which the world would recognise as:

> There were rats, rats, with bowler hats and spats
> In the quartermaster's store,

to 'For All the Saints' arranged by Vaughan Williams (Sine Nomine). This last was at Campbell put to a use considered almost blasphemous by my orthodox Presbyterian friends, to say nothing of me, at least while I still considered myself a born-again Christian, when it was sung always and only on the mornings of school-cup ties, carrying with it at least a hint that the saints and heroes adverted to were the members of the first fifteen, blessed in their non-playing captain.

Oh may Thy soldiers, faithful true and bold,
Fight as the saints, who nobly fought of old,
And win with them the victor's crown of gold.

And when the fight is fierce the battle long,
Steals on the ear the distant triumph song,
And hearts are brave again and arms are strong.

Thou wast their rock, their fortress and their might,
Thou, Lord, their captain in the well fought fight,
Thou in the darkness drear their one true light.

The golden evening brightens in the west,
Soon, soon to faithful warriors cometh rest,
Sweet is the calm of paradise the blest.

And so on. Wing three-quarters had never known so huge if wholly farcical a success. Second-row forwards had never looked so self-conscious.

It would certainly be true to say that you meet a nicer class of hymn in *Hymns Ancient and Modern* than you do in, say, *Gospel Bells* or *Alexander's No. 3* or *Sacred Songs and Solos* or the plain *Gospel Hymn Book* favoured by the Ulster brethren, in its red canvas cover with an acrostic featuring the brethren's favourite verse of scripture:

G od so loved the world that He gave His
O nly begotten
S on that whosoever believeth on Him should not
P erish but have
E verlasting
L ife.

Many of the upmarket hymns which I first encountered at school were quite unknown to the brethren, and when I imported them into the circle of my friends and relatives they were greatly admired, especially those at the more meaningless end of the sentimental spectrum:

> Unresting, unhasting,
> And silent as light,
> Nor wanting, nor wasting,
> Thou rulest in might.
> Thy justice like mountains,
> High soaring above,
> Thy clouds which are fountains
> Of goodness and love.

Or:

> O Sabbath rest by Galilee,
> O calm of hills above
> Where Jesus knelt to share with thee
> The silence of eternity
> Interpreted by love.

For whilst the brethren dearly loved a sentimental hymn, their best efforts were more often pitched at the level of:

> Come home! Come ho-ho-home!
> Ye who are weary come ho-ho-home!
> Softly and tenderly Jesus is calling,
> Calling, O sinner, come home!

Or, the natural antiphon:

> I am coming Lord,
> Coming now to Thee,
> Wash me, cleanse me in the blood
> That flowed on Calvary.

Or, at the nadir:

Jesus is our shepherd,
Wiping every tear,
Folded in His bosom,
What have we to fear?

Jesus is our shepherd,
For the sheep He bled,
Every lamb is sprinkled
With the blood He shed.

Or, perhaps not, for even when I remember something really awful, it always seems possible to recall something worse:

When my life-work is ended and I cross the swelling tide,
When the bright and glorious morning I shall see,
I shall know my Redeemer when I reach the other side,
And His smile will be the first to welcome me.

I shall know Him! I shall know Him!
When redeemed by His side I shall stand.
I shall know Him! I shall know Him!
By the print of the nails in His hand.

There He will be at the never-ending celestial reception, the cynosure with the paraclete on his shoulder and a shy smile across a crowded room, and somehow you will know, even then, that you are going to see Him again and again and again and again.

Friends will be there I have loved long ago,
Joy like a river around me will flow,
Yet just one smile from my Saviour, I know,
Will through the ages be glory for me.

Glory for me and glory for you, and the knock-down argument against all atheists and sceptics.

In comparison with hymns like these, John Greenleaf Whittier's almost palpable Galilean stillness, the love-interpreted silence of eternity, must, understandably, have seemed exotic. It should be admitted, however, that the brethren were less impressed by the equally unfamiliar, but genuine poetry of my school hymn book.

> He who would valiant be
> 'Gainst all disaster,
> Let him in constancy
> Follow the Master.
> There's no discouragement
> Shall make him once relent
> His first avowed intent
> To be a pilgrim.

Or:

> A man that looks on glass,
> On it may stay his eye;
> Or if he pleaseth, through it pass,
> And then the heaven espy.

Some sentimental favourites, at least as the world would classify these things, were firmly excluded from our hymnology. For example, 'The Old Rugged Cross' was never sung, not on the grounds that it was too syrupy by half but rather because, papist-style, it made an icon of the cross, diverting our attention from its proper object, the Crucified. I never heard 'Abide With Me' sung at a brethren meeting, perhaps because the last verse, 'Hold thou thy cross before my closing eyes', evoked a similar image of Last Rites and priestly trumpery. 'Lead Kindly Light' was not in our hymn books since it was surely not a kindly light which led its author, John Henry, Cardinal Newman, wherever it led him. 'Rock of Ages' was not much sung because the final verse seemed to suggest that it would be possible to seek refuge in the Rock of Ages at the last judgment, by which time it would of course be much too late.

> When I soar to worlds unknown,
> See thee on Thy judgment throne,

33

> Rock of Ages, cleft for me
> Let me hide myself in Thee.

We would not, however, have dismissed this famous hymn as Kingsley Martin did on the grounds that it was just another example of evangelical nonsense. 'Be of sin the *double* cure,' Martin sneered. What on earth, the sage of Great Turnstile wondered, was a double cure? However, the hymn goes on to spell out exactly what a double cure is: 'Save me from its guilt *and* power.' Indeed, the brethren went one better than Augustus Toplady, frequently eulogising in their prayers a triple cure, alliterative to boot, in that the blood of Christ had saved us from the Penalty of sin and was every day saving us from the Power of sin and would one day ('Thank God!') save us from the very Presence of sin.

A very large number of the brethren's hymns address those perennial evangelical themes, the apparent outsider who is really an insider, the temporally disadvantaged who will be eternally compensated, the short-term loser who is a long-term winner, the fool for Christ's sake, the last-laugher.

> Why should I charge my soul with care?
> The wealth in every mine
> Belongs to Christ, God's son and heir
> And He's a friend of mine.
>
> And when He comes, in bright array,
> And leads the conquering line,
> It will be glory then to say
> That He's a friend of mine.

Or:

> When you look at others with their land and gold
> Think that Christ has promised you His wealth untold.

34

> Count your many blessings money cannot buy,
> Your reward in Heaven and your home on high,

rewritten by at least one preacher in the straitened 1930s as:

> When you look at others with their motor cars,
> Dressed in fancy dresses like the fill-im stars.

It is surely the sigh of the oppressed creature (fancy dresses), but it is at once both smug and rather envious, and more than a bit vulgar. My friend Jesus's dad's a mine-owner. Yet are the sentiments expressed in these and innumerable other hymns so different from the rather more elegant endorsement by the author of the Epistle to the Hebrews (11:24–6) of a similar utilitarian calculation?

> By faith Moses, when he was come to years, refused to be called the son of Pharaoh's daughter; choosing rather to suffer affliction with the people of God, than to enjoy the pleasures of sin for a season; esteeming the reproach of Christ greater riches than the treasures in Egypt; for he had respect unto the recompense of the reward.

The brethren who, like most evangelicals, had a lot of respect for the recompense of the reward, relished ministry from passages like these which assured them of happy days soon to come at the end of the vale of tears – 'Earth's sad story, closed in glory'.

> Midst the darkness, storm and sorrow,
> One bright gleam I see.
> Well I know the blessed morrow,
> Christ will come for me.

Not that the faithful should merely sit back and anticipate the good times ahead, for, as the saints were often reminded, although each and every one was assured equally of his share of eternal bliss, nevertheless in heaven some of us would be more equal than others. Did we not have it on the authority of Paul himself that the post-salvation lives of some saints would amount to nothing more than wood, hay and stubble, while the lives of others would produce gold, silver and precious stones? The work of the latter would endure and be rewarded, whereas the work of the former would be burned, and although the lazy saint would be saved it would be so as by fire (1 Corinthians 3:12–15). Nor could it be assumed that the saints themselves were the best judges of what would in a coming day be revealed as gold and precious stones.

> Deeds of merit, as we thought them,
> He will show us were but sin.
> Little acts we had forgotten
> He will tell us were for Him.

The brethren, to a sister, were in good voice as they sang these familiar words, relishing the future comeuppance of some of our more spectacular preachers, upstaged by the humble at the final day, when that best portion of a good woman's life, her little, unremembered, nameless acts of kindness and of love would be recognised by the Saviour. How clearly, almost clairvoyantly, they could envisage the scene! 'That little thing, Lord? Sure, it was nothing, anyone would have done that. I had forgotten it altogether.'

At one of the brethren's large Easter conferences in the Grosvenor Hall in Glengall Street, a missionary brother on furlough, our man in Madras, was much admired for the following illustration. In India, we were told, they tell the story of a great maharajah who was once confronted in the marketplace by a poor untouchable with his begging bowl. The maharajah makes no contribution, saying, 'I am a great prince, what have you to offer me?' With a great show of contempt the beggar carefully picks out five grains of rice and gives them to the maharajah. In the evening, as he prepares his meagre supper, he sees in his bowl of rice a flash of gold. It *is* gold. One, two, three, four, five nuggets. No more. The mendicant twigs and groans,

'Oh, how I wish I had given him all.' And so our missionary is in sight of the peroration he has been working for. 'May God grant that no young brother, may God grant that no young sister in this great gathering tonight will have it to say on a coming day – "Oh, how I wish, how I wish I had given Him all!" '

> We lose what on ourselves we spend,
> We have as treasure without end
> Whatever Lord to Thee we lend.

A Portrait of the Young Christian as a Small Investor.

So it was not unnatural that after such sermons the brethren should conclude their meeting by singing:

> I shall wear a golden crown,
> When I get home.
> I shall lay my burden down,
> When I get home.

If the jingle seems unimpressive when compared with the passage from the Epistle to the Hebrews, the bathos must surely lie in the form rather than in the content.

Many years later, when I read Simone Weil's *Waiting on God* I wondered what the brethren would have made of it should they ever, attracted by its evangelical-sounding title, have come across it.

> All the circumstances of the past which have wounded our personality appear to us to be disturbances of balance which should infallibly be made up for one day or another by phenomena having a contrary effect. We live on the expectation of these compensations. The near approach of death is horrible because it forces the knowledge upon us that these compensations will never come.

No words from the most infamous of infidels, from Thomas Paine or Robert Ingersoll or Bertrand Russell, would read more chillingly, more opposed to everything the brethren stood for.

'These compensations will never come.' If they had been told that this writer, who urged that Christians if they were to be truly Christlike must rid themselves of their belief in and desire for compensations, either this-worldly or other-worldly, was esteemed by many as herself a most saintly Christian, they would have been incredulous, perhaps with some justification. As if compensation was not the point of it all. Like the apostle Paul in his letter to the Romans, the brethren 'reckoned', surely the *mot juste*, 'that the sufferings of this present time are not worthy *to be compared* with the glory that shall be revealed'. 'For our light affliction, which is but for a moment, worketh for us a far more exceeding and eternal weight of glory' (2 Corinthians 4:17).

'Do not be worried', read the modern translations of the Gospel According to John, chapter 14, 'In my Father's house are many rooms.' The brethren will be disappointed. They are expecting mansions.

> Therefore I'll murmur not,
> Heaven is my home.
> Whate'er my earthly lot,
> Heaven is my home.
> Danger and sorrow stand
> Round me on every hand,
> Heaven is my fatherland,
> Heaven is my home.

Our hymn tunes were sometimes jolly:

> I am feasting on the Living Bread,
> I am drinking at the fountainhead,
> For, whoso drinketh, Jesus said
> Shall never, never thirst again.
>
> What! Never thirst again?
> No! Never thirst again!
> What! Never thirst again?
> No! Never thirst again.

For, whoso drinketh, Jesus said
Shall never, never thirst again.

And sometimes they were melancholy-sentimental.

I've wrestled on towards Heaven,
'Gainst storm and wind and tide.
Now, like a weary traveller,
That leaneth on his guide,
I'll bless the hand that guided,
I'll bless the heart that planned,
When throned where glory dwelleth,
In Immanuel's Land.

Some were genuinely moving. Patricia Beer remembers, as I do, being touched (the chin-up tune helped) by the lines:

'Mid danger and fear, Lord,
I'm oft weary here, Lord.
O hasten the day
Of Thy coming again.
Thou art gone over there, Lord,
A place to prepare, Lord.
Thy joy I will share
At Thy coming again.

Some were well-written:

Sinners in derision crowned Him,
Mocking thus the Saviour's claim.
Saints and angels crowd around Him,
Own His title praise His Name.
Crown Him! Crown Him!
Spread abroad the Victor's fame.

I liked the opposition of 'mocking the claim' to 'owning the title', the natural, unforced rhymes, 'claim', 'name' and 'fame', the crowd scene where the Saviour is mobbed by Mr Bleaney, Mr Moses Bartholomew and the angels.

Some were aggressive and, it must be agreed, rather noisy.

Some were not strictly hymn tunes at all, but such as 'Drink to Me Only With Thine Eyes' or 'Flow Gently, Sweet Afton' with different words: 'I heard the voice of Jesus say' or 'I love Thee Lord Jesus I know Thou art mine'. One such borrowing had for me an interesting spin-off in later years. The hymn was one which, and this was unusual, I cordially detested. The words were a series of questions addressed to the sinner inviting him to consider his prospects in hell for all eternity should he die unsaved. The tune was neither aggressive nor melancholy-sentimental but an entirely dirge-like matching of sound to sense. I had no idea what this tune was, and, because in my post-brethren years I led a sheltered political life, it was not until the era of the televised party conferences that I re-encountered it. It was 'The Red Flag'. So what a joy then to turn down the sound just a bit and sing along with Tony and Shirley and Eric and Neil and Jim and Denis and Glenys and all the rest of the comrades:

> *Eternity, time soon will end*
> (The people's flag is deepest red)
> *Its fleeting moments pass away.*
> (It shrouded oft our martyred dead)
> *O sinner say, where wilt thou spend*
> (And ere their limbs grew stiff and cold)
> *Eternity's unchanging day?*
> (Their heart's blood dyed its every fold)
> *Wilt thou the hopeless horror see*
> (Then raise the scarlet standard high)
> *Of hell for all eternity?*
> (Within its shade we'll live and die)
> *Eternity, eternity,*
> (Tho' cowards flinch and traitors sneer)
> *Where wilt thou spend eternity?*
> (We'll keep the red flag flying here)

So I totter down cemetery road with a headful of hymns, sometimes fearful of ending up in a geriatric ward, chanting snatches of old lauds, listening to 'Songs of Praise' on the television and being condescended to by nurses who tell the visitors that 'he knows all the words'. I saw Mr Cliff Michelmore the other night when I dreamt that I was being interviewed by him for a job as one of the presenters of 'Songs of Praise'. I was successful. I would be guaranteed twenty programmes a year at a salary of £10,000 plus expenses. Not a great deal of money, said Michelmore. I was delighted. I would be able to take early retirement, swan about the country, Keswick, Ullapool, Painswick, Ilfracombe, Bettes-y-coed, Pitlochry, Ballyhalbert, Paignton, the pier at Mousehole in early autumn, a December afternoon in Ely Cathedral, and with my pension still be as well off as I am now, or better.

In my dream the scene seemed to change. I saw myself standing against a famous backdrop. It was the white cliffs at Dover, a perfect summer's evening, August for the people, and they stretched away on all sides, toddlers paddling in the shallows, their deckchaired parents and grandparents clutching hymn sheets. I was announcing the penultimate hymn:

> The day Thou gavest, Lord is ended,
> The darkness falls at Thy behest.
> To Thee our morning hymns ascended,
> Thy praise shall sanctify our rest.

The sea of faith gurgled in, islanding a few last figures in distant pools, and the massed bands of the Salvation Army sent up their long, melancholy roar. Then the vicar commended us all to the Lord in prayer, as the brethren would have it, and before the credits began to roll I had one more glimpse of myself, word-perfect without benefit of hymn sheet, singing my head off.

> O happy day, that fixed my choice
> On Thee my Saviour, and my God!
> Well may this glowing heart rejoice,
> And tell its raptures, all abroad.

41

Happy day! Happy day!
When Jesus washed my sins away.
He taught me how to watch and pray,
And live rejoicing every day.
Happy day! Happy day!
When Jesus washed my sins away.

For sounds and sweet airs like these I cried to dream again. I had not been so happy since Rita Hayworth slipped exiguous, scarlet knickers down her golden thighs and softly said, 'Dear heart, how like you this?'

But now the cosy parlour is long gone and in the houses the little pianos are closed. A clock strikes four and we all sway forward into the soundless dark.

In brethren circles the question must arise as to precisely what day was the happy day that fixed the young believer's choice on Christ his Saviour and his Lord. The preferred epiphany would be a moment of revelation inspired by some popular verse of Scripture:

> Romans ten and nine
> Is a favourite verse of mine,
> Confessing Christ as Lord,
> I am saved through grace divine.

'Matthew 11 and 28', 'John 5 and 24' and the perennial 'John 3 and 16' were also favourite verses gratefully remembered by many a saved sinner. The actual day of salvation, the brethren believed, being of Damascus Road significance must be etched forever in the memory, remembered exactly for its time, location and mode. Thus my grandfather was saved (1) on 5 August 1880, (2) while working in the fields and (3) through (as the brethren would put it) 'Romans 4 and 25'. My trouble, as I came under increasing psychological pressure to get baptised and come into the meeting, was that it seemed to me as if I had been saved at least a dozen times between the ages of seven and thirteen. Of course I was far too orthodox to say or even hint at such a thing, knowing that salvation was a once-and-for-all experience, and that a dozen happy days meant at least eleven, and possibly, dreadful thought, twelve false dawns.

Which day, then, was the day? I was, alas, at a preposterously early age, a victim of what the brethren called doubts. Not that the doubter, *qua* doubter, was necessarily unsaved. The happy day having been experienced and the great transaction done, Satan himself, or his minion Giant Despair, may insinuate doubts in the mind of the vulnerable believer leading him through the Slough of Despond into Doubting Castle. Some venerable saints, likely to be foot soldiers who did not actually speak out either as gospellers or as participants in the Lord's Day morning meeting, were often the object of some sympathy in this regard. Poor old Mr Bleaney, it might be said, nobody else doubts that he is saved but somehow he seems to lack the assurance. However, it is not easy at the age of nine to resolve the question, am I a saved doubter who lacks the assurance that he is saved or an unsaved doubter who never believed properly in the first place?

Young Gosse, who was inducted into the fellowship of the saints at an even earlier age than I, having been baptised on his tenth birthday, did not have to undergo the soulsearching which I invested in actually naming the day, the father having speculated that the son was one 'whom early training, separation from the world, and the care of godly parents had so early familiarised with the acceptable calling of Christ that his conversion had occurred, unperceived and therefore unrecorded, at an extraordinarily early age. It would be in vain to look for a repetition of the phenomenon ... The heavenly fire must not be expected to descend a second time; the lips are touched with the burning coal once, and once only.' Mark Rutherford records a similar exception to the rule when he was admitted to the assembly of Calvinistic Independents to which his parents gave their allegiance.

> It was the custom to demand of each candidate a statement of his or her experience. I had no experience to give; and I was excused on the grounds that I had been the child of pious parents, and consequently had not undergone that convulsion which those, not favoured like myself, necessarily underwent when they were called.

44

An unperceived, unrecorded conversion was not a ploy which would have been available to me, and I never heard it invoked in the case of any of the children of the believers, however young. With us a convulsion was *de rigueur*. If you claimed to be saved then you ought to know precisely when, where and how you were saved.

So Gosse having been, as his father put it, precociously selected, was spared my precocious doubts, all that stop-go, all those visions and revisions. These doubts of mine were of a highly linguistic, even philosophical turn, focused on the difficult concepts of 'belief in' and 'belief on'. In what exactly did those (were they distinct?) activities (were they actions?) consist? How exactly did you believe in or believe on the Lord Jesus Christ?

The concept of 'belief' *simpliciter* seemed to me an altogether more straightforward concept. Surely believing a particular proposition was not something that you did, but rather beliefs were something to be had willy-nilly, and, furthermore, by a simple act of introspection a person might discover for himself exactly what he believed. For example, I believed that Everest was the highest mountain, that the Battle of Hastings was won by William the Conqueror in 1066, that there were eight pints in an imperial gallon, that Winston Churchill was the Prime Minister, that *mensis* was the ablative plural of *mensa* and that Quito was the capital city of Ecuador. These were my true beliefs and furthermore I knew that they were. So I searched the Scriptures for a text which might allow that belief *that* so and so rather than belief *in* or belief *on* would do the trick. As related in the Acts of the Apostles chapter 8, the story of the eunuch who was Chancellor of the Exchequer to Queen Candace of the Ethiopians seemed to set a useful precedent. This eunuch, *en route* to the Gaza Strip, is puzzling over his Old Testament when he is joined by Philip of whom he asks regarding the sheep dumb before his shearer whether the prophet is speaking of himself or of another man. Philip expounds to him chapter 53 of Isaiah, explaining that this remarkable passage is indeed not about the prophet Isaiah but is about Jesus Himself: it is He who is the man of sorrows, acquainted with grief, taken from prison and from judgment, making His grave with the wicked but with the rich in His death. And I could look into my heart and affirm with complete sincerity that in this matter I agreed with Philip. The eunuch forthwith requests to be baptised. 'And Philip said, If thou believest with all thine heart, thou mayest. And he answered and said, I believe that Jesus Christ is the Son of God.'

Well, that seemed clear enough, no nonsense about believing in and believing on, but just believing that ... a fact. And I did. I did believe that Jesus Christ was the Son of God. But surely this was too simple. Only the heathen in their blindness, such as the Eskimos of Greenland's icy mountains and the Hindus of India's coral strand, and of course the Jews, believed otherwise.

The brethren distinguished between nominal Christians (our word for the great unwashed mass of Christendom) and real Christians or Christians *tout court*, sometimes to amusing effect. Thus, at the time of Dr Donald Coggan's elevation to the See of Canterbury, one of the more worldlywise amongst us was heard to remark with some satisfaction, 'I understand that the new Archbishop of Canterbury is a Christian.' The world, overhearing such a bizarre comment would doubtless have riposted jokily, 'Well, we didn't think he was a Sikh or a Buddhist', an ecumenical opportunity unlikely to be grasped this side of the third millennium. My worry was that all nominal Christians surely believed that Jesus was the Son of God. The Archbishop of Canterbury, whose salvation was at best problematic – it was many years before Dr Coggan – believed it. The Bishop of Rome, whose damnation was unproblematic, believed it.

What was the difference between believing in/on and believing that? Clearly, some believing in was nothing more than believing that. Believing in ghosts or believing in Father Christmas was nothing more than believing that there were such things as ghosts or that Father Christmas actually existed. So believing in Jesus Christ or believing in the Son of God might be construed as believing that Jesus Christ/the Son of God existed? To claim my salvation under an interpretation like that came uncomfortably close to invoking the warning of the General Epistle of James (2:19). 'Thou believest that there is one God; thou doest well: the devils also believe, and tremble.' Clearly there was a distinction between believing in and believing that.

One of the many differences between real Christians (like the brethren) and nominal Christians was that real Christians believed in both a personal God and a personal devil, while many nominal Christians, we were startled to learn, although they believed in a personal God, did not believe in the devil. However, our belief in the devil must in its turn be distinguished from a Satanist's belief in the devil. Where we merely believed that there was a devil the Satanist had (the word could no longer be evaded) faith in him. The Satanist trusted the devil. Did I trust the Lord Jesus Christ?

So, clearly, belief in Jesus Christ was akin to belief in sea air and fresh food, which was not just a matter of conceding that there were such things as ozone and spinach. But what was it to trust Jesus or put your faith in Him? The brethren were fond of the analogy in which the father tells the frightened boy to jump from a dangerous height assuring the child that he will catch him. The leap of faith was here reified. But just because it was reified it seemed useless to me as an analogy. Of course you put your faith in fresh air and sea food by becoming a consumer, in a shaky plank by stepping on it and in your father by jumping. But when you trusted in Jesus what did you actually *do*? Divorced from any particular deed, the act of faith, like Wittgenstein's act of will divorced from any real action, seemed to shrink to an utterly mysterious, extensionless point.

Wittgenstein was not a name that had much currency among the brethren of my formative years. Indeed, it is not unlikely that they, like George VI, as G. E. Moore was startled to learn from George VI himself, had never even heard of Wittgenstein. However, there is one insight of the great philosopher that I imagine the brethren would have endorsed, at least as that insight might be applied to the concept of faith. For the brethren were insistent that faith in Christ was not a matter of any introspectible feeling that the putative believer might claim to have had. 'Feelings will not save you' was actually a line in one of their hymns which set out a menu of non-remedies before concluding triumphantly, 'Faith in Christ will save you'. Any feeling would be compatible with a future state of affairs in which it transpired that the alleged conversion had not occurred at all, and therefore no feeling could be, in Wittgenstein's word, a criterion of conversion. And Wittgenstein had famously argued that understanding, as when we understand the meaning of a word or how to develop a simple arithmetical series like, 1, 5, 11, 19, 29 ... cannot be any introspectible feeling since any feeling will always be compatible with a subsequent misuse of the word or an incorrect development of the series. For Wittgenstein, of course, it is the subsequent practice, the use of the word or the development of the series within the linguistic or mathematical consensus which is the criterion of understanding. Here is a step which the brethren would have been loth to take: the criterion of faith and therefore of salvation would be nothing more or less than the lived life. Faith, like Wittgenstein's understanding, would not stop short of going on in the right way. The brethren would not have liked that because of the emphasis it seemed to place on works, and because they believed, without going so far as James Hogg's justified sinner, that from even a great deal of going on in the wrong way one could not necessarily conclude that the backslider was not a saint. And what about deathbed conversions? The dying thief was saved all right even though he had no opportunity to go on in the right way.

Such cogitations, amazing the troubled midnight and the noon's repose, may seem excessive to the point of being quite unrealistic. Nevertheless, that was how it was, and I was encouraged when I first read *Mrs Beer's House*, Patricia Beer's beautifully observed memoir of her days amongst the Torquay and Exmouth brethren of the 1920s and 1930s, to learn that she too remembers how in a panic she got saved every Sunday, 'trying frantically to go through the process thoroughly and in a way that would leave no loophole, though the mechanics of "believing on the Lord Jesus Christ" and accepting his offer of Salvation were like catching a train in a nightmare'. That is how I remember it: the mechanics.

Well then, was I saved or not, and if so, where, when and how was I saved? The questions were asked more and more frequently and with, it seemed to me, increasing exasperation. My mother, who was good at making me feel sorry for her with consequent guilt, was pained and embarrassed by my vacillations. Kindly evangelists were scrupulous in the duty visits they paid us, thereby acknowledging that 'Pure religion and undefiled before God and the Father is this, To visit the fatherless and widows in their affliction ... ' (James 1:27). 'Is the lad saved yet?' they would never fail to ask in my presence, and my mother would have to admit that although I had professed to be saved at Mr So-and So's last series of special gospel meetings, I had subsequently disavowed as a result of doubts.

This distinction between professing to be saved and actually being saved was one to which the brethren were very much alive. Even the fondest mothers were canny, and for months after their sprig's alleged conversion would respond to any enquiry into the state of his soul only with, 'Well ... he professes, but time will tell.' I remember Aaron Bartholomew, son of Moses, a more than ordinarily creepy young preacher who, while giving his testimony, would often refer to this twilight

49

state between profession and full acceptance into the fellowship of the Lord's people. Erstwhile worldly companions he had of course given up ('come out from among them, and be ye separate', 2 Corinthians 6:17):

My old companions, fare ye well!
I will not go with you to hell.
I mean with Jesus Christ to dwell.

Now those same old companions would mock him in the street, shouting after him, 'Hey! Professor! Are you all right, Professor?' and he would think (he said), Could they be right? Is it possible that I am not all right with God? Could it be that I am not truly saved, that I am after all only a professor. Since he was of a pale, clerkly mien, with granny spectacles, his breast pocket packed with not less than five fountain pens and propelling pencils, even the brethren were mildly amused at his confusion.

In my case, the thing was far beyond a joke; there had been altogether too many professions. Ah well, the visiting evangelist would say sadly, 'Shall we have a wee word of prayer and speak to God about it?' And down on our knees we would go, the preacher and I, his arm round my thin shoulders, my mother, because of her injuries, being allowed to remain seated. 'Dear heavenly Father, we bring before Thee Max, this child of many prayers … '

I would clearly have to fix a date. It could be any, though not of course all of a number of occasions, for I knew I could go right back to the very first time I had professed and claim to realise (with assurance) that of course that had been the day all the time. So was it 27 August 1939, at nine o'clock, on Ballyholme beach, at the closing session of a CSSM (Children's Special Services Mission) campaign, after my sandcastle, with its complicated system of moats and drainage, had won second prize in the competition for survival against the evening tide? After the sausages and the icecream, after the choruses:

> I am travelling on the Hallelujah Line
> On the good old gospel train,
> I am on the right track, and never will go back
> To the city of Sin again.
> I pay no fare, I'm travelling on a pass,
> 'Tis the Lamb for sinners slain,
> I am travelling on the Hallelujah Line
> On the good old gospel train.

And then more seriously:

> He lives! He lives!
> Christ Jesus lives today.
> He walks with me, He talks with me
> Along life's narrow way.
> He lives! He lives!
> Salvation to impart.
> You ask me how I know He lives
> He lives within my heart.

After this, the English evangelist, so much softer than our homegrown Ulster species, cajoling in the twilight, urging that not one of us there that summer evening was too young to ask the Lord Jesus to come into his or her heart:

> I'm not too young to trust in Jesus
> For He loves a little child.

He pleading with us to remember our Creator in the days of our youth, before the grinders ceased because they were few, before those that looked out of the windows were darkened, before the grasshopper became a burden. 'So let us all sing together!':

> Wait not till the shadows lengthen
> Till you older grow.
> Rally now and sing for Jesus
> Everywhere you go.
> Lift your joyful voices high,
> Singing clear through earth and sky,

51

Let the blessed tidings fly!
Jesus lives!

And so I went home in an emotional buzz and for the first time told my mother and father that I now was saved. What my story was I can no longer remember exactly but it would certainly have included as essential elements that I had realised, aged seven, that, young as I was, I was a guilty sinner who deserved to go and was indeed going to hell and the Lake of Fire for ever and ever but that Jesus having suffered instead of me (the just for the unjust) I had invited Him into my heart and was now assured that I was going to heaven 'should I die that very night'. As a way of putting it the cardiac invitation would be the only concession to my youth. Otherwise this was the orthodox package to which any adult would be expected to subscribe and with which I had been thoroughly indoctrinated by my elders, who were surely more mad than bad.

Conversion under the auspices of non-brethren like the Children's Special Services Mission was quite acceptable; many a well-thought-of brother tied his conversion to the preaching of some Baptist or even some Presbyterian, usually distinguished from the run of the mill by being referred to as that 'Godly' Baptist or Presbyterian. Nevertheless, five years later, I wondered if mine was quite the thing.

Perhaps I was saved at the more mature age of twelve, at teatime on the afternoon of the annual Sunday school trip to Portrush and the Giant's Causeway. At this time I was under the spell of a lovely girl called Grace Magowan who at fourteen and a half was already saved, baptised and in the meeting, and who could play 'The Sweet By and By' with variations which involved lots of arpeggios and much crossing of her hands. She had taught me to sing 'Guide me, Oh Thou Great Jehovah' (with parts), *cwm rhondda*-ing away just like Cardiff Arms Park.

Bread of Heaven, Bread of Heaven,
Feed me now and evermore.

Grace Magowan was of course rather more sophisticated (she was after all fourteen and a half) than the infant Gosse who put out his tongue at the unbaptised children of the believers, sitting at the back of the room outside the privileged circle of communion, to remind them that he now broke bread as one of the saints and they did not. Nevertheless, her attitude towards me was one of hardly concealed condescension, and the masochist in me found it not unpleasant. So as we picnicked together at the White Rocks on jam doorsteps and currant buns out of a bag, I wanted to be saved too, for I would certainly have to become her brother if I was ever to be her husband. A sentimental soul, stuck in that adolescent treacle of bibles and billets-doux, I would sing to myself:

Amazing grace, how sweet the sound,
That saved a wretch like me.

Or, even worse:

'Twas grace that taught my lips to pray,
And made my eyes o'erflow.
'Tis grace hath kept me to this day,
And will not let me go,

thinking *Grace* for *grace*. Well then, four o'clock at the causeway through Ephesians 2 and 8, 'For by grace are ye saved through faith; and that not of yourselves: it is the gift of God'. But surely I could not have got saved for the sake of a pun.

The question was still unresolved when my mother and I were invited to go to stay, for the Christmas of 1945 and into the New Year, with my father's cousin in Strabane. The visit was fraught with embarrassment, for it was my first since I, an unhappy, ungrateful, indeed a disgusting evacuee in my cousin's house, had left under a cloud considerably bigger than a man's hand. It is hard to say to what extent guilty memories of my anti-social practices precipitated my latest and last conversion. However, it was at least appropriate that the miserable sinner of 1942 should return to be saved for the last time at the scene of his crimes.

During the year following the air raid I had first gone to live with my uncle, my father's brother, a farmer at Ballywillwill, County Down, and then, in 1942, with my father's cousin, a prosperous smalltown draper, in Strabane, County Tyrone.

While at Ballywillwill, I attended, with my young cousin, the Roman Catholic, two-room, two-teacher school at Clanvaraghan, an institution so primitive that I, a nine-year-old incomer from a public elementary school in the great metropolis of Bangor, County Down, was considered a prodigy. I carried all before me, winning the all-school spelling bees, when my orthodox spelling of such words as 'yacht' was preferred to the 'yots' and 'yatts' of great lumpen fourteen-year-old girls. The country marvelled, but my mother worried that the environment was not improving my chances of ever realising her ambition for me by becoming qualified to be a doctor in darkest Africa under what our medical missionaries called a hotter sun.

I doubt that my mother's qualms about my education give the real reason for my removal in less than six months from Ballywillwill to Strabane, where I lasted only a further six months. The truth is that these no doubt well-intended exercises by my relatives in Christian charity were not entirely successful, as is evidenced by the speed with which I became *persona non grata* in both households. Doubtless I was difficult, exhibiting traits which were not becoming in a child who had at least professed to be saved at least twice. How much this year contributed to the chronic anxiety in which I have lived the rest of my life, the angst (remorse about the past, guilt about the present, anxiety about the future) I was delighted to discover ten years later in Cyril Connolly's symptom book, *The Unquiet Grave*, I could not say. It surely helped me to acquire that proper sense of sin and alienation from God which Bobbie Wright found so sadly wanting in the untutored Japanese.

> There is a city bright,
> Closed are its gates to sin,
> Nought that defileth, nought that defileth
> Shall ever enter in.

On my ninth birthday, just exactly a month before the bomb, my father had given me his second-best hunter watch. Not having a waistcoat, I wore it proudly in the breast pocket of my blazer, suspended from the lapel by its dazzling chain. I consulted it frequently.

This watch, which I was quite sufficiently in love with in the month before my father was killed, took on a new significance after his death. It was now 'his father's watch', 'his father's last birthday present to him' and as such often commented on by my sentimental elders – 'something he will surely always cherish'. There will be psychologists who would not be too surprised to learn that by the time I arrived in Strabane I had started to drop the watch, sometimes on a hard floor. The watch stopped. Had I dropped it? No, it had just stopped. It was taken to the jeweller to be repaired. Then it stopped again. Had I dropped it? No. It was repaired and on the following Sunday in the gloomy passageway which led from the dining room to the *en suite* shop my father's cousin confronted me. The jeweller had reported that the watch's injuries were consistent with its having suffered a substantial jolt and indeed were inexplicable otherwise. So I might as well own up. When did I last drop my father's watch? I demurred, or I suppose the word is wriggled. Then I suddenly capitulated. Was it not wicked to be so careless with my father's watch which should mean so much to me and then to compound the felony by lying about it? Yes. And the first time it stopped, you dropped it then too? No, honest, that time it just stopped. You know that's not true, you dropped it, didn't you? Yes.

Although I was nine years old I shared a bedroom with my cousin's sister-in-law, a spinster who was manageress of the shop and, like other members of that extended family, to me an honorary aunt. That this accommodation was necessary in that large house I find hard to believe. It was perhaps thought that I would be in need of surrogate mothering. That idea is supported by the story I was often told of how excited and pleased 'Auntie' Matilda had been by the prospect of my coming, so much so that she had decorated her room and with her own hands made new matching curtains, pelmets and bedspreads out of bright materials hard to obtain in time of war. These gruesome honeymoon arrangements are not pleasant to contemplate.

This lady found it hard to get me out of bed on schoolday mornings, and became irritated at the contrast between my weekday lethargy and the alacrity with which I could be up and about on Saturdays. On Saturdays the lure was the shop where friendly assistants allowed me to climb ladders to fetch down the boxed shirts and blouses and to put the customer's money into a wooden ball and with a tug send it singing along the high wires to the cashier's eyrie. One gossipy shopgirl broke for me the code by which my cousin indicated on each ticket the wholesale price of the merchandise ... 'Don't you say I told you!' I didn't – more deviousness. The key was the word *righteously*, which with its eleven letters provided all that was necessary for the £ s. d. of the time. Thus £47 10s. 11d. was ho/l/y, and £8 3s. 4d. was u/g/h and the stratagem a nice example of that combination of commerce and piety for which the brethren have sometimes been thought notorious. With such a code the retail mark-up could hardly have been excessive?

So, really in order to teach me a lesson, but ostensibly so that by being compelled to have a lie-in on Saturdays I should be more wideawake on Mondays to Fridays, 'Auntie' Matilda decreed that on Saturdays I should stay in bed until ten o'clock. On the second Saturday I was very fidgety by half past nine and at twenty minutes to ten I helped the hour hand on and got up. When I was discovered up and about before the appointed time I protested that the clock in our bedroom showed ten o'clock before I got up. Had I moved it? No. But it might be going fast. This episode obviously excited some discussion, for a few days later my cousin summoned me. He had performed an experiment. At exactly twelve o'clock on Tuesday he had wound up and set our clock as the town hall clock was chiming. On Wednesday at twelve o'clock he went back to our room (Matilda's and mine) and lo and behold the hour hand touched twelve exactly as the town hall clock started to chime. What had I to say to that? After some ineffective shoulder play to the effect that it was a mystery, beyond me, I conceded that I had indeed interfered with the clock. Downright disobedience covered up by more lies.

My troubles were not all horological. On weekday mornings a poor boy from a slum off Railway Street would call at the shop to accompany me to school. As well as being poor he was deformed, suffering from some form of spasticity. I don't know who was supposed to be doing whom a favour, Arnie Robertson to me for the interest he was taking in the poor orphan come into our midst, or me to him for what I would have thought more obvious reasons. Certainly I resented him for his Uriah Heepish ways, his mangled speech and his persistent dribble. My guardians encouraged the relationship on the grounds that he was an occasional attender at the Sunday school who it was hoped might become a regular and even be won for Christ through our association. He was to be one of the wee chums about whom we sang on Sunday afternoons.

Bring your wee chums to the Sunday school,
Tell them to come round and see us.
Tell them it's only from three to four
The stories are all about Jesus.
Jesus, the sinner's friend,
Oh, what a wonderful story.
He'll keep you to the end,
That you may be with Him in glory.

There was some annoyance within the circle of my benefactors when I did my best to avoid Arnie.

One day I was summoned to a family conference. Arnie, whom I now managed to evade most days at least on the homeward walk from school, had come into the shop and told 'Auntie' Matilda that I had called her a bad name. He had told her what the name was. Would I like to be a brave boy and confess to what I had called her. Then we could ask God to forgive me for the Lord Jesus Christ's sake? I protested, for a change with complete sincerity, that I had no idea what I was supposed to have called her. After some chivvying I was offered a prompt. 'It begins with a B.' I was alarmed. Could I, I had certainly forgotten, but could I have called her a bastard? Or perhaps a bitch? And which would be worse? (Bitch, I was inclined to think.) That old bastard/bitch won't let me get up on Saturday mornings? I shook my head. I could not bring myself to confess to either. The members of the panel shook their heads too, but gravely, in utter amazement at such stubborn depravity (wagging their heads, it suddenly struck me, just like the mockers, 'they that passed by', in the New Testament). Then, moving in for the kill, someone suddenly said, 'B ... U.' I was relieved and then puzzled. Not bitch. Not bastard. But what? More head-shaking, mystified on my part, solemn on theirs. 'B ... U ... G.' I seized on this with some enthusiasm. To be sure, all memory of the expletive had been deleted, and it did seem an odd sort of pejorative. But surely it was not gravely sinful? The old spider,

59

the old flea, the old daddy-longlegs, the old bug, how dare she keep me locked up in her room?

'Yes,' I confessed, eyes decently lowered. 'I did call her an old bug. I'm sorry.'

But this was not right either. The wagging went on, slower than ever, so many metronomes stuck in adagio. 'You are a very bold, devious little boy.' (In Ulster dialect 'bold' when applied to small children is not the opposite of 'sly' or 'secretive' or 'devious'.) 'You know very well you didn't call her that. A bug, indeed! It was *B* ... *U* ... *G* ... *G* ... *E* ... *R*. You called her a bugger, didn't you?' With hindsight it must seem improbable that Matilda was a bugger, and at the time my incomprehension was sufficiently obvious to give the inquisitors pause. 'What is a bugger?' I dared to ask, but answer came there none.

After that, it was downhill all the way. I had been forbidden to walk home by the canal which was said to be dangerous, and indeed there had been a drowning during the previous winter. Of course I continued to do so and managed to get myself found out by the quite extraordinary expedient of dropping one of my shoes into the deep, slimy water. I came home half shod, claiming to have lost a shoe, but when, where and how I could not say. Arnie, however, who had been tagging along, was able to supply the facts.

Then I started to behave in a way that nearly fifty years later I find it hard to think about. I began quite deliberately to foul myself. I might be having tea with my relations on a visit to some brethren family, when, instead of asking to go to the lavatory I would quite deliberately start to shit, there where I sat at the tea table. Or I would be in the morning meeting at the back of the room with the other children while the brethren broke bread, a non-communicating spot at their feast of charity, a raging wave of the sea foaming out his own shame (Jude 13). There was no urgency. I could have waited. There was no sphincter failure. The action was voluntary and yet in the very performance I was appalled and frightened at what I was doing. Then I would walk about in that shameful state for the rest of the day, awaiting the inevitable discovery. The maids who had to do the washing were disgusted, the family was disgusted, I was disgusted, indeed horrified at the way I was behaving. Yet I did it again and again.

The idea that our actions may be driven by desires and motives which never rise to the level of consciousness is not as fashionable as it once was. Freud is no longer a whole climate of opinion and the modish attitude towards him, at least in some philosophical circles nowadays, inclines more to ridicule that to reverence. Nevertheless, puzzled by this episode, I cannot but feel drawn towards a psychoanalytical explanation. How was it possible to behave quite deliberately in a way I passionately wanted not to behave? Every night I prayed that I would not do it again, much as a bedwetter might pray for an end of his enuresis. But that makes sense, for the bedwetting is something the delinquent suffers rather than an action he performs quite deliberately, however Freud might try to soften that common-sense distinction. Could an analyst bring it all back and make me understand (and accept) how and why I 'really' wanted a state of affairs which I consciously abhorred, I would have said, with all my being?

It was all too much. My poor mother, with more than a year in hospital behind her and another year still to go, brought me back to Bangor and installed me in a boarding house on the Hamilton Road, a hundred yards from the Tonic cinema. It was out of season and I enjoyed my almost adult status, breakfasts and high teas with the transient reps and the permanents among whom there was a pretty schoolteacher who made much of me – reading till all hours what had ante-bellum been forbidden fruit, the *Hotspur*, the *Wizard*, *Skipper*, *Champion* and the *Rover*. The landlady did not see it as part of her contract to be a mother or even an 'aunt'. Immediately my behaviour became socially acceptable, that of an ordinary house-trained nine-year-old.

For some years after, I would regularly pray that God would enable me to keep myself clean, for Jesus Christ's sake, amen.

To Strabane, then, I returned more than three years later, still a guilty, foul, unclean, wash-me-Saviour-or-I-die, hell-deserving sinner, and one Sunday evening I was more than ordinarily terrified by an effective piece of hellfire oratory. I cannot think why this particular effort should have done the trick. It is unlikely to have been anything out of the way in either manner or matter, for although our evangelists were wont from time to time to deplore the Laodicean times we lived in – claiming to remember a golden age of preaching in their youth to say nothing of the youth of their fathers and their fathers' fathers when, as they thundered, there were giants in Israel, faithful servants of Christ who were not afraid to preach heaven or hell, turn or burn – they would invariably go on to demonstrate that they themselves were in no way deficient in these oldtime virtues. There was not one of them who did not pride himself on his delivery of a sound, no-punches-pulled message, what they called preaching a good gospel.

The subject of this particular oratory was the second coming of the Lord, one potent to strike fear into the hearts of the well-indoctrinated children of the believers. Soon, soon the day was coming when the very last soul would be saved and Jesus Christ would return to the air to call his waiting people home.

God's house is filling fast,
Yet there is room,
Some soul will be the last,
Yet there is room.

I could see myself only five places from the head of the queue when the 'HOUSE FULL' notices went up outside God's house.

The scenario would be nicely detailed by our more imaginative preachers. A saved bus driver would be caught up to heaven just as he was negotiating the hairpin bend on a 1 in 7 incline. A born-again signalman would be taken while express trains converged at great speed in the direction of unswitched points, the consequent collision the least of the unraptured travellers' worries. A Christian surgeon would leave his patient opened up and a Christian patient would leave his surgeon openmouthed. Yet within weeks, so we were assured, such were the soporific powers of the Prince of Darkness, the world would have forgotten or explained away the startling circumstances of the day when the salt was taken out of the earth.

Often in the past, under the influence of such preaching I would awaken early in the night, convinced by the silence of the house that the Lord had come, and then creep down the stairs to be reassured by voices from the sitting room that God's house was not yet full and my time was not yet up. Such experiences were common in evangelical households and were frequently attested to by the frightened children themselves when in due course they got saved and related the story of their conversion from the gospel platform. ('The Lord in His great mercy had often spoken to me in the past, sometimes waking me from deep sleep with the conviction that He had come again and taken my loved ones to be with Him in the Glory, leaving me behind to face the just and righteous judgment of a Holy God.') Now, at thirteen years old, I was not above being scared by the prospect of the empty graves, the sheeted dead, friends and relations caught up in the air to be forever with the Lord, the circle irreparably broken, the children of many prayers left behind to face their inevitable and richly deserved punishment.

Too late! Too late! will be the cry,
Jesus of Nazareth has passed by.

64

Peter Waring, the eponymous hero of Forrest Reid's novel, tells a similar story of terrors which faded only when his father told him that all the Jews must return to Jerusalem before the last day. ('Now there was a Jewish family living in Castlewellan that I thought I could keep my eye on.') Such advice was not available in our circle, where the unexpectedness of the Lord's return, like a thief in the night, was a constant threat. 'Then shall two be in the field; the one shall be taken, and the other left ... Watch therefore: for ye know not what hour your Lord doth come' (Matthew 24:40–42) – a threat at least to the unbeliever who would be left, but a promise to the believer for whom the sky not the grave was the goal. As preachers with a reputation for humour would put it, we looked not for the undertaker but for the uppertaker. Edmund Gosse tells us that his father on retiring for the night would often say, 'with a sparkling rapture in his eyes, "Who knows? We may next meet in the air, with all the cohorts of God's saints!"' So it was with us. The Lord's return was constantly and confidently expected 'perhaps this very night'. The Epistle of James (5:8) was ever present in our mind: 'the coming of the Lord draweth nigh'. Confronted by the last-day scoffers of whom Peter writes, who said, 'Where is the promise of his coming? for since the fathers fell asleep all things continue as they were', the brethren would argue, more ingenuously than ingeniously, that if the second coming was drawing nigh nearly two thousand years ago, how much nearer must it not be tonight? And anyway, as they would quickly, if somewhat inconsistently, point out, 'one day is with the Lord as a thousand years, and a thousand years as one day' (2 Peter 3:8), this latter verse surely suggesting that the Lord's promise might be kept and his near return not unreasonably be expected within a week of his departure in say the year AD 6400.

In such a fashion then it came about that an evangelist pointed me to the Lord Jesus Christ for the very last time and, as the brethren would put it, I closed with God's offer of salvation, citing the Epistle of James chapter 5 and verse 8 as the instrument of my awakening, and the prophecy of Isaiah chapter 53 and verse 5, 'But he was wounded for our transgressions, he was bruised for our iniquities: the chastisement of our peace was upon him; and with his stripes we are healed', as the instrument (under God) of my salvation – sound, middle-of-the-road, conservative texts, somewhat lacking in originality. The preacher, who was staying at my cousin's house for a month of special gospel meetings, looked well pleased with the night's business.

This cousin, the brother of Bobbie Wright of Japan, now restored to his labours, ministering to the Japanese recusants and snatching further souls from the eternal flames, was, as I have said, a draper, prosperous enough to employ two maids in his house together with a nursemaid for his small children. She was pretty, pert, sixteen, and a few days after my final conversion I found myself in her bedroom where she kissed me, putting her hand into my shirt and caressing my nipples, encouraging me to reciprocate. Her breasts were beyond belief springy, a tactile datum of such novelty that I was speechless and it was indeed some years before I discovered the *mots justes* – pneumatic bliss.

I was at once charmed and appalled – saved on Sunday and a sex maniac on Wednesday. That would be scanned. I confessed to my mother and to the preacher that I was once again having doubts, though not of course the precipitating cause of the doubts. My mother was already, as I say, wearied with my propensity over the last few years to declare myself saved one week only to have doubts the next. And the preacher was not in the mood to see his good work for the first cousin once removed of a valued patron so quickly undermined. So I was talked out of my doubts, in effect told to pull myself together. In consequence, it became official that I was saved through Isaiah 53 and 5 in the Gospel Hall, Railway Street, Strabane, at 28 minutes to 9 on

Sunday 29 December 1945, my happy day, though not so happy as the following Wednesday.

Not many weeks later I remained behind after the Sunday evening gospel meeting in order to be interviewed by Mr Moses Bartholomew and Mr Gibson Stevenson and an assortment of lesser elders, with a view to being baptised and then admitted into their fellowship. Young Edmund Gosse so charmed his interviewing panel, brothers Fawkes and Bere, that on his introduction to the communion 'each strove to exceed the other in the tributes which they paid to my piety. My answers had been so full and clear, my humility … had been so sweet, my acquaintance with Scripture so amazing, my testimony to all the leading principles of salvation so distinct and exhaustive, that they could only say that they had felt confounded, and yet deeply cheered and led far along their heavenly path …' My performance cannot have been so virtuoso since Mr Bartholomew reported to the assembled saints only that the brethren had been 'satisfied' as to where, when and how I had been led in trusting faith to accept the Lord Jesus Christ as my own and personal Saviour.

'My public baptism,' writes Gosse, 'was the central event of my whole childhood. Everything, since the earliest dawn of consciousness, seemed to have been leading up to it. Everything afterwards seemed to be leading down and away from it.' I cannot remember my own baptism as being so remarkable an apogee. Rather, once I had got myself saved for the very last time, there seemed to have been a sort of tedious inevitability in my progression through conversion (after conversion after conversion) to baptism and reception into the assembly of the saints who met at the Knightsbridge Gospel Hall, Sunshine Street, Belfast, a poor thoroughfare running through a maze of lower-middle-class housing. So that when the evening actually came round and I sat through my last Sunday evening gospel meeting as an unbaptised believer, I experienced that feeling, so familiar to those of a fatalistic turn of mind, of being in the grip of forces and events over which I had no control. I was doing the done thing.

On the occasion of Gosse's baptism people flocked from near and far, from Exeter, Dartmouth and Totnes, to see the prodigy. The proceedings were further enlivened by a young woman who, having been herself denied baptism, either stumbled or threw herself into the tank before the official business had got under way. This episode occasioned some debate among the brethren as to whether she had in the will of the Lord achieved a baptism *malgré les autres*. Gosse senior denied that this was so, on the rather absurd grounds that her head had not been immersed, when he might with greater plausibility have insisted that any baptism requires that there be both baptised and baptiser. For my part, I was perhaps stumbling into baptism, though not literally.

On that April evening, nothing so out of the way made my initiation memorable and the audience was no more than the regular attendants at the gospel meeting, the local saints, their as yet unsaved children and a sprinkling of unsaved friends doing an embarrassed favour to the saint next door who had plucked up the courage to invite them to come and hear the gospel. The gospel hall was its familiar, shabby self, no fixed pews but only movable benches, the walls decorated with familiar texts, 'Where two or three are gathered together in my name, there am I in the midst of them' (Matthew 18:20), 'Be ye also ready' (Matthew 24:44), 'Prepare to meet thy God' (Amos 4:12), 'While we were yet sinners, Christ died for us' (Romans 5:8), all painted onto *trompe-l'œil* 'scrolls' by which no eye had ever been deceived, the weak spring sunshine dribbling into the hall through windows innocent of stain.

The only difference from an ordinary gospel meeting, one which made the scene rather more squalid than usual, was that underneath the platform and at the feet of the front row of the congregation, which had been moved back to clear the space, the floorboards had been lifted to reveal a large tank, 7 feet by 4 and 3 feet deep, full of grey, stagnant water. During the hour-long meeting it lay directly under my eyes, the site of my fast-approaching embarrassment.

For now I was embarrassed. Although my last (agreed) conversion was as recent as last December so that I should have been in the days of my first love (Revelation 2:4) I already blushed to think what school friends like Simmons or Spender or Barry or Nightingale would say, were they to see me here, now, like this. Or my cynical housemaster whose lip seemed to curl when I had to ask permission to go unsupervised on Sunday mornings, not with the *bien élevés* to either the parish church of St Mark at Dundela or to the Presbyterian church at Belmont, but to the Ballyhackamore Gospel Hall; not even to church at all but only to a meeting. Less than a year ago I had been happy to make a spectacle of myself by declining (as a Christian) to join in a school visit to a cinema in celebration of the Allied victory in Europe. Now I coloured at the memory of the gesture, fully recognising that I would no longer be courageous or foolhardy enough to repeat it. It was not that I did not believe, only that I was most reluctant to bear witness in the company of unsympathetic outsiders to the truth that was in me, this reluctance being itself probably an indication that it was not. Like young Gosse, a self-confessed coward who let sleeping dogmas lie, I was beginning 'more and more to keep my own religion for use on Sundays'. It seemed likely that from now on I would be, like Joseph of Arimathea, a disciple of Jesus, but secretly, in my case for fear of the Episcopalians. Not an auspicious start.

Like Gosse again, I 'never urged the Atonement' on my school friends. I shuddered, quite literally, at the very thought of having to use the word 'saved' in my friends' hearing - 'By the way, Nightingale, I would like to tell you that I am saved. I wonder are you saved?' - foreknowing that the very concept must seem to them more vulgar than incomprehensible. The expression *non-U*, later popularised by Nancy Mitford, was not available in 1946. Had it been, I would have been in no doubt that 'saved' was about as *non-U* as 'dentures', toiletpaper' and 'pleased to meet you' and that a saved Mitford was not so much an empirical impossibility as a conceptual absurdity.

When not many years later I first read Thornton Wilder's *Heaven's my Destination* and came upon the exchange between that importunate innocent, George Brush, and a stranger on a train – 'Brother, can I talk to you about the most important thing in life?' 'If it's insurance, I got too much, if it's oil wells, I don't touch them and if it's religion, I'm saved' – I laughed out loud, at least in part because of a shocked realisation that there were actually people who knew all about being saved and thought the very idea risible.

At the close of the gospel meeting the preacher announced that there would now be a short baptismal service which all, whether saved or unsaved, were invited to stay and witness. To my dismay, everyone, even unsaved friends wearing lipstick, decided to stay to see the show. There were not to be, however, among these friends any counterparts of the Irish quarryman John Brooks and his wife Ann, who, having come to mock young Gosse, remained to pray and went away so impressed that they were shortly afterwards saved, baptised and breaking bread with the Oddicombe saints, a happy outcome for which Edmund understandably took some of the credit. Thereupon, having read some appropriate passages of Scripture including the one about the Ethiopian eunuch which I had rejected as providing too facile a rite of passage, Mr Bartholomew said he would now say a few words, and did.

We were gathered here this evening to witness our young brother following the Lord in baptism. It was not that baptism was necessary for salvation as the Roman Catholics were falsely taught, otherwise the dying thief would not be in heaven today which praise God he was.

> There is a fountain filled with blood
> Drawn from Immanuel's veins,
> And sinners plunged beneath that flood
> Lose all their guilty stains.
>
> The dying thief rejoiced to see
> That fountain in his day,
> And there have I, though vile as he,
> Washed all my sins away.

Not that in the first place what the Roman Catholics or indeed even the Protestant so-called churches practised was baptism at all since 'baptise' meant to immerse. From the Greek. We would recall that the eunuch we had just been reading about went *down into the water*. When our blessed Lord Himself was baptised we read of Him that He went *up out of the water*. When you went down into the water and when you came up out of the water that did not mean sprinkling, friends. And now this evening our young brother has satisfied the elders of this assembly that he has indeed, as a guilty hell-deserving sinner, put his whole faith (that word again) in the atoning death on Calvary of our Lord Jesus Christ and has been saved for all eternity and we thank God this evening for that. Baptism, important though it is, could not have saved our young brother, and I hope there is no one in our meeting this evening who is putting their faith in baptism or sprinkling or confirmation or any of the rites of the so-called churches for the salvation of your eternal soul. It's too important, sinner friend. It's far too important. As some of you may know I myself was brought up in the so-called Church of Ireland. As an infant I was sprinkled by the local rector and when I was twelve years old I was confirmed by the Bishop of Connor. I tell you my friends when I was twelve years old I was *confirmed* all right. Oh yes, what I was was a confirmed sinner on my way to hell and the Lake of Fire, that's what I was. I needed to be saved and no amount of sprinkling or confirming could ever have accomplished that, indeed no it could not. When the great earthquake broke down the doors of the gaol where Paul and Silas had been imprisoned we read that the gaolkeeper trembled and said to Paul and Silas, 'Sirs, what must I do to be saved?' And they said 'Believe on the Lord Jesus Christ and thou shalt be saved.' And he believed and washed the prisoners' stripes and was baptised straightaway. Friends, that is God's order. If you're going to be baptised you had better get saved first.

The speaker having done his duty by the friends through providing a second helping of the gospel now addressed the saints on the more recondite question of the meaning of believers' baptism. Baptism was a symbol of the believer's participation in the death and resurrection of Jesus Christ. As the great apostle to the Gentiles wrote in his Epistle to the Romans, 'Know ye not that so many of us as were baptized into Jesus Christ were baptized into his death? Therefore we are buried with him by baptism into death: that like as Christ was raised up from the dead by the glory of God the Father, even so we should also walk in newness of life', Romans chapter 6, verses 3 and 4. By being baptised this evening our young brother was saying to the world out there, the world that crucified and still crucifies the Lord Jesus Christ, that he is now dead with Christ. The flesh, the old Adam is crucified with Christ. Remember that Christ, being found in fashion as a man, humbled himself when he became obedient unto death, even the death of the cross, Philippians, 2 and 8. The shame of it! To the Greeks foolishness but a stumblingblock to the Jews, First Corinthians 1 and 23. For remember brethren, in the eyes of the world there will be reproach. By being baptised our young brother will share in the reproach of Christ. The world despises those Christians who have had the courage to identify themselves with the crucified One in an act of public baptism. Dippers, they will say, with a sneer on their lips. (Simmons! Pinder! Barry! Nightingale! Taffy Ragg! 'Dipper' Wright was a nickname I felt I could live without.)

But then there was the other great truth of baptism. For three days and three nights our blessed Lord lay in the garden tomb of Joseph of Arimathea, in that new sepulchre wherein was never man yet laid. But on the third morning the stone was rolled away and Christ was raised from the dead by the glory of God the Father. So just as baptism tells us that we are crucified with Christ so it tells us that nevertheless we live and moreover we live to walk with Him in newness of life, old things having passed away and all things being now new. Our young brother this evening is a new creature in Christ Jesus. Second Corinthians 5 and 17. It is our sincere prayer to God that he will dedicate his young life to the service of the Son of God, the Man of Calvary who loved him and gave His life for him and that he will be long spared to follow in His blessed footsteps. Shall we pray?

Our loving, Heavenly Father, we thank Thee this evening for the death, burial and resurrection of Thine only begotten Son, our Lord and Saviour, Jesus Christ. We thank Thee that although we were as sheep gone astray, turned everyone unto his own way, without any merit that could have commended us to Thee, but only a certain fearful looking for of judgment and fiery indignation, Thou, God, commended Thy love towards us in that while we were yet sinners Christ died for the ungodly. We thank Thee oh God for everyone under this roof this evening who can look back to the day and hour when in simple faith they put their trust in the atoning work of Calvary. No work of ours could ever have sufficed.

> Not the labour of our hands
> Could fulfil Thy laws' demands.

It is by grace that we are saved and that not of ourselves, it is the gift of God, not of works, lest any man should boast.

> In which no work of mine has place,
> Else grace with works were no more grace.

Then we would thank Thee Lord for those loving hands which took our blessed Saviour down from the tree and laid Him in Joseph of Arimathea's new tomb. And we thank Thee Lord that Thou didst not suffer Thy Holy One to see corruption, that death could not keep his prey, that Thou Oh God didst tear the bars away and on the third day Thou didst send Thine angel to roll away the stone and Thou didst raise Him from the dead. Dear Lord, we thank Thee that Christ is today our risen Saviour, seated at Thy right hand, ever living to make intercession for us. For if Christ be not risen we are of all men most miserable. But He is risen and we are not miserable. Like the disciples of old on that blessed resurrection morn we are glad because we see the

Lord. We live because He lives, and one day in the not too distant future we shall live and reign with Him. For we look for that blessed hope, which we have as an anchor of the soul both sure and steadfast, and the glorious appearing of the great God and our Saviour Jesus Christ. As the hymn writer has put it so beautifully:

Living, He loved me,
Dying, He saved me,
Buried, He carried my sins far away.
Rising, He justified,
Freely for ever,
Some day He's coming, Oh glorious day!

We would commend to Thee very specially this evening our young brother who this evening will shortly pass through the waters of baptism. Lord, Thou hast saved him and we thank Thee from the bottom of our hearts for that. Now, with full acknowledgment of the solemnity of the occasion he has intimated to the oversight his desire to follow Thee in baptism, by which he will signify that he is now dead to the things of the world, being risen to walk with Thee in newness of life. For if we have been planted together in the likeness of His death, we shall be also in the likeness of His resurrection, knowing this, that our old man is crucified with Him, that the body of sin might be destroyed, that henceforth we should not serve sin. Look over him in the coming years that he may serve Thee in all things and never dishonour the precious Name of the One who called him from darkness into His marvellous light, that he may always press toward the mark for the prize of the high calling of God in Christ Jesus, so that he may in a coming day hear from those blessed lips those most beautiful of words, 'Well done, thou good and faithful servant!' All these things we ask in the Name and for the sake of our Saviour, Jesus Christ, Amen!

The prayer over, I was escorted by some of the elders to a

cloakroom behind the platform where I was clad in an anklelength nightshirt weighted at the extremities, with my swimming trunks as an additional insurance against the possibility that, Ophelia-fashion, my clothes would spread immodestly wide and garland-like. While this was going on the congregation was singing a hymn popular on, and perhaps written for, such occasions. The verses which alluded to the burial aspect of baptism were sung in a low, growling, clods-on-the-coffin manner, and the chorus in which the resurrection motif was introduced, was sung in contrasting, bright and chirpy staccato. While I was robing, the congregation sang only the gloomy verses.

> Low in the grave He lay,
> Jesus my Saviour,
> Waiting the coming day,
> Jesus my Lord.
>
> Vainly they watch His bed,
> Jesus my Saviour,
> Vainly they seal the dead,
> Jesus my Lord.
>
> Death could not keep its prey,
> Jesus my Saviour,
> He tore the bars away,
> Jesus my Lord.

No further procrastination was possible. I emerged from the cloakroom to walk the few yards to the tank and climb down the steep steps into the water, my skirts smoothed round my ankles by the senior elder who was waiting for me in rubber boots with leggings and a high bib, like a sewage worker or possibly a working-class angler. Mr Strange was the manager of the Irish Temperance League tearooms in Cromac Street, a saint highly esteemed for his knowledge of the Word, who had himself been converted under the ministry of that man of high degree, heavenly-minded all could see, my grandfather. In consequence, he had always taken a fatherly interest in the orphaned grandson of his father in Christ. Well pleased then by the evening's business, my John gripped me firmly by the chest and the small of the back (a sensitive manoeuvre with the young sisters) and addressing me by name intoned; Robert Maxwell Wright, on the confession of your faith I baptise thee in the name of the Father and the Son and the Holy Ghost. The confusion of vocatives was entirely typical. 'I baptise thee' was obligatory but 'thy faith' would have sounded precious. So down I went, unlike Edmund Gosse's exhibitionist competition, right under, thoroughly dipped, and up I came, spluttering and blinded, to be hauled out by the waiting elders with their towels. The congregation then broke into the chorus they had been saving for the dénouement.

> Up from the grave He arose,
> With a mighty triumph o'er His foes.
> He arose a victor from the dark domain
> And He lives for ever with His saints to reign.
> He arose! He arose!
> Hallelujah! Christ arose!

Hearing them, I was conscious of an ambiguity similar to that at Campbell on cup-tie mornings, when the First Fifteen more than half believed that they were the saints who, captained by Jesus in the well-fought fight, would shortly rest from their labours. A mighty triumph o'er his foes? A victor from the dark domain? Me! As V. S. Pritchett says of Gosse's baptism, nothing could have been more dingily farcical.

Gosse was young enough not to be embarrassed by the dingy farce, young enough indeed to take some pride both in his immersion and in his consequent status as a communicating saint. Surely one of the most felicitous passages in *Father and Son* is his description of Philip's confusion when in the following year the widower admits to his son that he is proposing marriage with an unbaptised lady.

> I remembered that it was my duty to testify 'in season and out of season'. I therefore asked with much earnestness, 'But, Papa, is she one of the Lord's children?' He replied, with gravity, that she was. 'Has she taken up her cross in baptism?' I went on, for this was my own strong point as a believer. My father looked a little shame-faced, and replied: 'Well, she has not yet seen the necessity of that, but we must pray that the Lord may make her way clear before her. You see, she has been brought up, hitherto, in the so-called Church of England.' Our positions were now curiously changed. It seemed as if it were I who was the jealous monitor, and my father the deprecating penitent. I sat up on the coverlid and shook a finger at him. 'Papa,' I said, 'don't tell me that she's a pedobaptist?'

A few years older than Gosse, I could not share his enthusiasm, either at the time or subsequently. However, such embarrassment if it is to be suffered is perhaps best suffered young. On the rare occasions in later life when I was present at the baptism of a mature adult, I felt a vicarious embarrassment even more intense. Gosse says of his stepmother, 'a shy and sensitive lady of advancing years', who in the end submitted herself to a public immersion she regarded with horror, 'No wonder my stepmother was sometimes fretful.' Patricia Beer's father too was not a cradle brother but like the second Mrs Gosse an Anglican who had married into the assemblies. For some years he resisted the pressure to join, but eventually, having been blackmailed out of smoking he was bullied into fellowship.

> It was a summer evening, and he was carrying a change of clothes rolled up in a towel, an unpleasantly fraught version of someone going bathing. My mother did not accompany him, on the pretext of having to stay and mind us, but she stood looking out of the window, as I so often saw her do, and watched him bicycling down the lane. She said: 'There's Daddy going to get baptized', and I felt embarrassed and ashamed.

There were bibles everywhere in those days. I can remember brethren evangelists who, when preaching the gospel, would refer, with some show of genuine grief in the face of such hardly imaginable deprivation, to unprivileged households in which there was not even one bible. I could understand their dismay, coming as I did from a home in which there were perhaps thirty-seven bibles, big bibles, small bibles, fat bibles, thin bibles, pocket bibles, family bibles, thumb-indexed bibles, bible-in-a-bag bibles, zip-fastener bibles, Lord's-prayer-on-a-postage-stamp bibles, all bound in bible-black goose flesh.

Orthodox brethren saw no need for any book other than The Book, with, for the scholarly, such backup material as might be provided by Cruden's concordance and pious commentaries. History, as they were fond of remarking, was His story. For the brethren were what Matthew Arnold called Hebraists, for whom no word of praise could ever be sweeter than 'He certainly knows his Bible.' They would not have taken kindly to Arnold's response, 'Whenever we hear this said, we may, without any elaborate defence of culture, content ourselves with answering simply: "No man who knows nothing else knows even his Bible."'

My mother had a taste for edifying fiction, for Mrs Swan, Mrs O. F. Walton, Miss Amy Le Feuvre and the authors of the Lily Library, which was, as she herself recognised, a weakness. She would never have read these excellent women on the Lord's Day. There was something wrong with a saint for whom the

Holy Bible was not sufficient. I was frequently reminded of the great privilege, which I shared with the infant Timothy, of constant exposure to the Word of God, 'that from a child thou hast known the holy scriptures, which are able to make thee wise unto salvation through faith which is in Christ Jesus' (2 Timothy 3:15). And indeed it is a privilege, one of the very few, I would say, consequent on such an upbringing. I cut my teeth on Genesis, I lisped in Numbers.

Edmund Gosse tells us that his father, before he had reached middle age 'had committed practically the whole of the Bible to memory, and if started anywhere, even in a minor prophet, he could go on without a break as long as ever he was inclined for that exercise'. Such expertise seems to us now remarkable to the point of being hardly believable. Imagine being offered the random prompt 'These are the horns which have scattered Judah, Israel and Jerusalem' and being able to pick it up without a pause: 'And the Lord shewed me four carpenters. Then said I, What come these to do? And he spake, saying, These are the horns which have scattered Judah, so that no man did lift up his head: but these are come to fray them, to cast out the horns of the Gentiles, which lifted up their horn over the land of Judah to scatter it' (Zechariah 1:19–21).

I could not with any confidence claim that my mother's competence in the Scriptures was on anything like that level, though certainly it was in its own way impressive, being based on a reading of the entire book, from Genesis to Revelation, every year for the best part of sixty years. This regimen would of course have been supplemented by much more frequent readings and re-readings of all the Gospels and the Epistles, of the more familiar parts of the Pentateuch and of the historical books, the psalms and the more popular prophecies, Isaiah and Daniel and the Revelation of Saint John the Divine, which was the material of much private study, as well as of public exposition at meetings and conferences.

When I officially resigned my doubts, got baptised and was admitted into the fellowship of the saints who gathered together in the Lord's Name at the Knightsbridge Gospel Hall, Sunshine Street, I too embraced the discipline of the yearly read which involved, as I remember, three chapters on weekdays and four chapters on Sundays. During the whole of the first year I was enthusiastic about the exercise. In the middle of the second year it began to pall. I noted with some initial dismay that I was glad to get into the Book of Psalms where three short chapters occupied less than a page (Psalm 119 being an irksome exception) and could be read in five minutes. Like Edmund Gosse, I could not but remark the contrast between my enthusiasm for secular literature and the 'increasing langour', as he puts it, with which I approached the daily passage. Saved a little over a year, I could not hide from myself that I was a good deal less keen on the minor prophets than on such blockbusters as *My Son! My Son!*, *Hatter's Castle*, *Gone with the Wind*, *King Cotton* and *Angel Pavement*. In a further year's turning, I realised that even Matthew, Mark, Luke and John seemed lacklustre compared with *Brighton Rock*, *Howards End*, *Black Mischief*, *The Dead Seagull*, *Hangover Square* and *Goodbye to Berlin*, worldly books indeed, so very much worldlier than my mother's suspect fare, *Teddy's Button* and *Jo's Boys* and *Elsie Dinsmore* and *Winsome Wins Through*.

Gosse comments: 'Of course, although I did not know it, and believed my reluctance to be sinful, the real reason why I found the Bible so difficult to read was my familiarity with its contents. These had the colourless triteness of a story told a hundred times.' Gosse's subsequent explanation that his reluctance was not sinful because the material was familiar would, I feel sure, not have satisfied him at the time of his disaffection and shows only how far he had slipped away from the old paths. Such an explanation would certainly have struck me as being dependent on a false antithesis. The familiarity of the material would not make the reluctance to read it any the less sinful. For age should not wither nor custom stale the infinite variety of the books of the Chronicles of the Kings of Israel. To the true believer the Word of God was the living bread, always new, manna to the hungry soul delivered fresh every morning.

The children of Israel, it will be remembered, sinned when they despised the manna and yearned for the fish and cucumbers of Egypt, for 'the melons, and the leeks, and the onions, and the garlick'. 'But now our soul is dried away: there is nothing at all, beside this manna, before our eyes.' They were not to be excused on the grounds that forty years of manna was boring. On the contrary, the anger of the Lord was kindled greatly against the people who wept for flesh rather than the manna He had provided which was 'as coriander seed, and the colour thereof as the colour of bdellium'. And so the Lord at first teased the jaded ingrates by dumping quails from the sea, two cubits high for miles in all directions round the camp. Quails for supper! 'And the people stood up all that day, and all that night, and all the next day, and they gathered the quails: he that gathered least gathered ten homers ... And while the flesh was yet between their teeth, ere it was chewed, the wrath of the Lord was kindled against the people, and the Lord smote the people with a very great plague. And he called the name of that place Kibroth-hattaavah: because there they buried the people that lusted' (Numbers 11:5–34). If that was the proper treatment for those who got fed up with manna after forty years, how should one be served who, after only thirty months, preferred *Cakes and Ale* to the Bread of Life? To have explained my staleness in Gosse's manner would not have been in any way to condone it, but rather to convict myself of sin, the root of the matter having in all likelihood never been there in the first place.

I love to tell the story
For those who know it best
Seem hungering and thirsting
To hear it like the rest.

> And when, in scenes of glory,
> I sing the new, new song,
> It will be the old, old story
> That I have loved so long.

At best, then, my langour was evidence that like the church at Ephesus I had lost my first love (Revelation 2:4):

> Tell me the same old story,
> For I forget too soon.
> The early dew of morning
> Has passed away by noon.

A more serious possibility was that I had early joined the ranks of the Laodiceans, and being lukewarm was like to be spued out of the Lord's mouth (Revelation 3:16). Most serious of all was the possibility that I had never been saved in the first place.

In the third year my appetite for the Word of God began to wane somewhere around the First Book of the Chronicles. 'Ezer the first, Obadiah the second, Eliab the third, Mishmannah the fourth, Jeremiah the fifth, Attai the sixth, Eliel the seventh, Johanan the eighth, Elzabad the ninth, Jeremiah the tenth, Machbanai the eleventh. These were the sons of Gad.' Not even speculation as to why Gad, with such a wealth of exotic names at his disposal, had called both number five and number ten Jeremiah, could make this sort of thing exciting, and by the time I reached the prayer of Habakkuk the prophet upon Shigionoth ('O Lord, revive thy work in the midst of the years!'), I was ready to concede defeat, the prophet's prayer unanswered.

When I questioned the wisdom of a yearly reading of the books of the Chronicles, with their tedious (not my word – I would not have dared) genealogies, I was reminded of a great preacher of my mother's youth who, at conference time, had raised that very question. He, so the story went, had as a young believer doubted the benefit to be had from a reading of the entire Word of God, especially the 'Eleazer begat Phineas, Phineas begat Abishua, Abishua begat Bukki and Bukki begat Uzzi' bits. Then, on the very morning that Satan first introduced that doubt into the young saint's mind he came in his daily reading to 1 Chronicles 4:9–10, a small oasis among the 'begats', where he read: 'And Jabez was more honourable than his brethren: and his mother called his name Jabez, saying, Because I bare him with sorrow. And Jabez called on the God of Israel, saying, Oh that thou wouldest bless me indeed, and enlarge my coast, and that thine hand might be with me, and that thou wouldest keep me from evil, that it may not grieve me! And God granted him that which he requested.' What a wonderful, wonderful prayer, the famous evangelist exulted, and what a marvellous answer from our great and loving God, and to think that he would have missed it if he had succumbed to temptation and not persevered with his daily reading. Very well, I proposed, then having discovered this prayer might he not mark the spot and in subsequent years come to it more economically, ignoring the 'begats'. The proposal was not conceded, on the grounds that it would detract from the surprise and delight which would attend a less calculated rediscovery of the passage. As with the landscape gardener of Peacock's *Headlong Hall*, unexpectedness was what we were aiming for. I did not at the time have to hand Mr Milestone's response: 'Pray sir, by what name do you distinguish this character, when a person walks round the grounds for the second time?' but the thought was there.

It must be conceded then that I unnecessarily expended a good deal of spirit in the wastes of the books of Chronicles and the minor prophets. Not all of these latter are tedious, of course, for while Zephaniah is surely not a jolly book, Jonah was great fun and is still well worth a yearly reading, along with *The Great Gatsby, A Handful of Dust*, 'The Dead', *The Unquiet Grave, The Diary of a Nobody, Heaven's my Destination, Murder in the Cathedral* and the rest of the old favourites.

The pace of Jonah is fast. The Lord tells Jonah to go and preach against Nineveh, a wicked city, but Jonah has other ideas and runs away to sea. The Lord pursues him with a mighty storm for which Jonah admits his culpability to the frightened crew, who then ditch him. The great fish swallows him and vomits him up on dry land three days later. (This famous episode was often referred to at the brethren's conferences because of its unique value as an indicator of the entirely commendable lengths to which the simple believer's faith could and should stretch without snapping. Thus our preacher would relate the story of the clever young clergyman ['a modernist'] who condescends to poor old Minnie ['my dear woman!'], protesting that she cannot possibly believe, cannot possibly *swallow* ['Ho! Ho!'] a story like that. Minnie stoutly replies that indeed she can ['sir!'], and furthermore ['sir!'] if God had told her in His own inspired word that Jonah had swallowed the whale she would believe that too. A susurrus of approval greets the umpteenth recitation.) So Jonah hotfoots it to Nineveh and preaches its destruction in forty days. The people repent and the Lord spares them. Jonah is furious and retreats to the suburbs where he builds himself a booth to sulk in. The Lord makes a gourd grow up to shelter him but, whimsical as ever, destroys it the next day and sends an east wind and strong sun so that Jonah faints with headache. The Lord asks Jonah if he does well to be so angry and Jonah replies that he does well to be angry even unto death. And the Lord says, 'And should I not spare Nineveh, that great city, wherein are more than sixscore thousand persons that cannot discern between their right hand and their left hand; and also much cattle?' End of story, end of book. As Joyce's Mr Crofton might have said: It is a very fine piece of writing.

I am glad, then, for the discipline which compelled me when I was young to search the Scriptures, even for all those innocent Bible games and Bible jokes with which we amused ourselves on Sunday evenings. Who was the wisest man in the Bible? Solomon. Who was the oldest man in the Bible? Methusalah.

Who was the strongest man in the Bible? Samson. Who was the shortest man in the Bible? Bildad the Shuhite. Who, apart from Melchisidec, had neither father nor mother? Joshua the son of Nun.

We played a game called Bible endings, adapted by me from the 'geography endings' played at school after lights out, and thought entirely suitable for Sunday evenings. Someone would start the game by mentioning a proper name (person or place) from the Bible, the next player had to follow with a name beginning with the letter with which the first name ended, and so on. Three misses or repeats and you were out, any hesitation of more than thirty seconds counted as a miss. So away we go. Jude, Elisha, Abraham, Moses, Silas, Sarah, Ham, Mordecai, Isaac, Caleb, Boaz, Zadoc, Claudia, Ahab, Balak, Kish, Heber, Rehoboam, Manasseh, Haggai, Israel, Luz, Zacchaeus (who, like some worldly Christians allegedly far too much interested in worldly newspapers, could not see Jesus for the press), Samaria, Apollos, Saul, Leah, Haman, Nebo, Obadiah, Herod, David, Dorcas, Seth, Hiram, Miriam, Moab, Bileam, Magog, Goliath, Habakkuk, (*K* was difficult) Keturah (Who? – Abraham's second wife, of course), Hazelelponi, Isaac (Had it already – one life gone), Ishmael, Lot, Tamar, Rahab, Bartimaeus, Simeon, Nebuchadnezzar, Rebecca, Aquila, Amos, Samson, Nimrod, Dives, Solomon, Nod, Dan, Nepheg, Gad, Didymus, Silvanus, Salem, Martha, Alexander (Not in the Bible – Yes it is: 'Alexander the coppersmith did me much evil', Second Timothy, 4 and 14), Rimmon, Nebat, Thyatira, Absolom, Mizpah, Hermogenes, Samuel, Laodicea, Antioch, Hadoram, Mephibosheth, Hosea, Abinadab, Baalam, Midian, Nathan, Nazareth, Hod, Deborah, Hagar, Ramoth-gilead, Demas, Shadrach, Heshbon, Nadab, Bedad, Damascus, Sara, Ananias, Syntiche, Eunice, Epaphroditus, Sheba, Amalek, Kibroth-Hattaavah, Hebron, Nabal, Lydia, Arphaxad, Darius, Sidon, Naomi, Isaiah, Hagab, Baal, Laban, Naaman, Naboth, Horeb (Are places allowed? – Of course they

are, we've already had Nazareth and Salem ... *You* had Nebo –
Is Nebo a place? – Oh! Nan! Don't you remember Nebo's lonely
mountain? Where Moses was buried? – Well then Horeb, *B*,
Beelzebub – Oh! Nan!), Boanerges, Sapphira, Abana, Abigail,
Luke, Ezekiel, Levi, Iscariot, Thomas, Sodom, Magdalene, Eve,
Esau, Urbane, Elizabeth, Hur, Rachel, Lebanon, Nahum, Merab,
Bethlehem, Malachi, Issachar, Reuben, Noah, Hannah, Harum,
Molech, Hammedatha, Abiram, Michal, Lod, Dathan, Nain,
Nathaniel, Lazarus, Sosipater, Rufus, Stephen, Nun, Ner, Ruth,
Hophni, Ira, Adam, Melchisidec, Crispus, Shiloh, Hermes,
Shechem, Macedonia, Asher, Rameses, Sisera, Aphses, Sinai,
Iddo, Onesimus, Satan, Nymphas, Smyrna, Aaron, Nicodemus,
Sardis, Shem, Melita, Abednego, Onan (Oh! Nan!).

I am especially grateful for the time when I read the Good
Book right through two and a half times. George Orwell, writing
more than forty years ago, claimed that people then did not
know even Bible stories: one could make the same case *a fortiori*,
I should think, in 1990. Consider a random list of fairly elementary scriptural references and ask yourself would they all be
familiar even to fairly well-educated people today. The new
Jerusalem and the old Adam, the fiery furnace and the chariot of
fire, Gideon's fleece and Aaron's rod, lean years and fat years,
the silver cord and the golden bowl, bowing in the House of
Rimmon and ploughing with Samson's heifer, the ring-straked
and the speckled, the ark of the convenant and the mark of Cain,
Elijah's mantle and Abraham's bosom, the road to Damascus
and the road to Emmaus, brothers' keepers and Job's comforters,
rivers of Damascus and waters of Babylon, the great white
throne and the still small voice, the good wine last and the last
first, the golden calf and the fatted calf, sounding brass and
tinkling cymbal, the hem of his garment and the latchet of his
shoe, the keys of the kingdom and the locks of Absolom, the
walls of Jericho and the streets of Askelon, Urim and Thummin,
Naaman's leprosy and Naboth's vineyard, Mary and Martha,

the mote and the beam, the den of lions and the plague of locusts, through a glass darkly and eyeless in Gaza, the daughters of the Philistines and the sons of thunder, wolves in sheeps' clothing and angels in disguise, Sibboleth and Ichabod, Abana and Pharpar, bulls of Bashan and swine of Gadara, two measures of barley for a shekel and two sparrows for a farthing, virgins without oil and bricks without straw, the pearl of great price and the stone which the builders rejected, Anathema Maranatha and Mene, Mene, Tekel Upharsin, stony ground and rough places, Pharaoh's daughter and Potiphar's wife, Baalam and Balak, Uriah the Hittite and Bildad the Shuhite, the burning bush and the brazen serpent, the widow's cruse and the widow's mite, the cities of the plain and the lilies of the field, behemoth and leviathan, Solomon's penis and Rehoboam's pinkie, Ahab and Rahab, Bethel and Bethany, the widow of Nain and the witch of Endor, answering a fool according to his folly and not answering a fool according to his folly, Delilah and Deborah, the tower of Babel and the cave of Adullam, stony hearts and feet of clay, the pillar of cloud and the pillar of salt, Castor and Pollux, the wisdom of serpents and the innocence of doves, Belshazzar's feast and Esau's breakfast, new wine in old bottles and butter in a lordly dish, the mammon of unrighteousness and the abomination of desolation. I imagine that the ten-year-old Gosse would have thought the task of writing short notes on all of them embarrassingly elementary.

Even some writers of great distinction seem unfamiliar with the Scriptures to a degree that anyone brought up amongst the brethren would find surprising. Thus Sean O'Faolain, in his book *The Vanishing Hero*, writes at some length of the inventive genius which Evelyn Waugh displays just in creating the title *Vile Bodies*. He speculates this way and that on its provenance, its subconscious origins, without a nod of recognition in the direction of Philippians 3:21: 'Who shall change our vile body, that it may be fashioned like unto his glorious body ...' Of course

O'Faolain belongs to a generation of Irish Catholics that was forbidden to read the Bible. At least, so we were told, though I imagine in these ecumenical days the Irish hierarchy will be allowed to protest successfully that it was always a Protestant slander. Fortunately, in the interest of what is the case, we have the vigorous testimony of Professor Stanislaus Joyce that it is not and was not. In *My Brother's Keeper* he recalls one of his teachers expounding the lines:

> Through the sad heart of Ruth, when, sick for home,
> She stood in tears amid the alien corn.

Dempsey, the teacher, knowing full well that his pupils have not read the story in the Bible, 'assumes' that they have, and the class, hypocritically, consents. Joyce comments:

> But, of course, we did not know the story and had never seen a Bible at home. Dempsey, for his part, knew what everyone in Dublin and perhaps in Ireland knew then and knows now, that in Catholic homes and in Catholic schools the Bible is never read ... Dempsey's candid presumption of basic, all-round hypocrisy irritated me chiefly because, although the question was not addressed to me, I had let it pass. I afterwards wished I had said out bluntly that I had never opened a Bible, and that I had always been led to regard it as a Protestant book.

Consider too, the case of Orwell himself. In 1940, Orwell wrote the famous essay in which he takes another smack at Auden, Day Lewis, Connolly and company ('the typical literary man ... an eager-minded schoolboy with a leaning towards Communism') by contrasting them, to their great detriment, with the egregious pornographer Henry Miller. (Orwell, for all his celebrated common sense, could, in his own way, be silly enough.) Orwell gave this long essay the title 'Inside the Whale', which surely indicates the importance he attached to the central passage in which he suggests that:

> Miller ... is inside the whale. All his best and most characteristic

> passages are written from the angle of Jonah, a willing Jonah ...
> He has performed the essential Jonah act of allowing himself to be
> swallowed, remaining passive, *accepting*.

Now this metaphor in its turn is by Orwell built on the idea that being swallowed by a whale must be a powerful folk wish because actually there is no biblical authority for such an idea. According to Orwell:

> Here Miller is touching upon what is probably a very widespread fantasy. It is perhaps worth noticing that everyone, at least every English-speaking person, invariably speaks of Jonah and the *whale*. Of course the creature that swallowed Jonah was a fish, and is so described in the Bible (Jonah 1:17), but children naturally confuse it with a whale, and this fragment of baby-talk is habitually carried into later life ... For the fact is that being inside a whale is a very comfortable, cosy, homelike thought.

However, had Orwell been slightly better read in Scripture, the conceit would surely not have got off the ground since he would have known that the whale/fish substitution was not based on baby-talk and Jungian folk fantasy but gets its authority from Jesus himself. 'For as Jonas was three days and three nights in the whale's belly: so shall the Son of man be three days and three nights in the heart of the earth' (Matthew 12:40).

Edmund Gosse came to think that he had been introduced at too early an age to the 'melodious language ... the forensic audacities' of the Epistle to the Hebrews. But I am not so sure. The melody lingers on, surviving childish incomprehension.

> For the law having a shadow of good things to come and not the very image of the things can never with those sacrifices which they offered year by year continually make the comers thereunto perfect ... If therefore perfection were by the Levitical priesthood, (for under it the people received the law) what further need was there that another priest should rise after the order of Melchisidec, and not be called after the order of Aaron? For the priesthood being changed, there is made also of necessity a change also of the law.

I may not have recognised the audacity but I believe I responded to the tune.

Besides, as Gosse says and I also remember, it was not all forensic audacities. There was the Book of Revelation where we, like Gosse, 'in our lighter moments chased the phantom of Popery through its fuliginous pages'. Gosse observes, and finds in me an answering chord, that his early immersion in that remarkable book so influenced him that in later years, when he met 'stout Protestants, gallant "Down with the Pope" men from County Antrim and ladies who see the hand of the Jesuits in every public and private misfortune', his feeling always was that 'their denunciations erred on the side of the anodyne'. Who, having learned at an impressionable age that the Roman Catholic Church is 'the great whore that sitteth upon many waters, a golden cup in her hand, full of abominations and filthiness of her fornication', a woman 'drunken with the blood of the saints and with the blood of the martyrs of Jesus', upon whose forehead is written, in capital letters, no less, 'MYSTERY, BABYLON THE GREAT, THE MOTHER OF HARLOTS AND ABOMINATIONS OF THE EARTH', is ever likely to forget?

Then there was the Beast, whose number was six hundred, three score and six. What did that mean? We should be told and frequently were. And all this would be supplemented by the Book of Daniel whose exact prophecies of happenings to be unfolded in the very near future seemed to me even more thrilling. When at our large Easter conferences in the Grosvenor Hall in Glengall Street some great preacher would invite us to open our bibles at the Book of Daniel I held my breath, and was extremely disappointed if it was only some tame stuff about the faith of the prophet who dared to stand alone in the den of lions, confident that the Lord would shut their mouths.

What I much preferred to hear about were the doings of the king of the north and the king of the south and the ram which had two horns and the two horns were high but one was higher than the other and the higher came up last , of the ram which pushes westward and northward and southward until it comes up against the he-goat with a notable horn between his eyes which breaks the two horns of the ram and waxes exceedingly great until in turn its great horn is broken and out of it grow four horns towards the four winds of heaven. And out of one of these horns grows a little horn which waxes exceeding great towards the south and towards the east and towards the pleasant land. All of this, ram, goat, great horn, lesser horn, little horn, south, east, west, was of the utmost significance and signalled to the brethren an apocalypse of horror and destruction soon to be set in train by nameable and indeed named nations. 'The elements shall melt with fervent heat' (2 Peter 3:10). A decade before Hiroshima and Nagasaki the brethren proposed that the king of the north and the king of the south would be armed with weaponry capable of destroying the entire globe.

There was also the great image of Nebuchadnezzar's dream, always a firm favourite with the brethren. From golden head and silver breast, through brazen belly and ferrous legs, he deteriorates to feet part of iron and part of clay. He represents the vainglorious empires of men, ourselves about to enter the pedestrian age whose defects will shortly bring the whole structure crashing down, gold, silver, bronze and iron transmuted into the chaff of the summer threshing floor. This age would be the age of what the brethren called the Revived Roman Empire and in the 1930s they looked forward to, that is to say, predicted, a united Europe made up of the ten nations of the old Roman empire and represented by the ten toes of the clayey feet. Many years later when the European Community came into being I watched its progress with some interest, thinking how the brethren must be rubbing their hands with delight as we entered the last days. The community for a while seemed to stick at nine members and now has grown to twelve or thirteen. Doubtless the brethren will have a plausible explanation for the supernumerary toes.

When, some years after my baptism, I was the only pupil at Campbell College to take Scripture in the Oxford and Cambridge Higher Certificate, I had the benefit of one-to-one instruction from a Presbyterian classicist with an interest in theology, who not only shocked me by taking the liberty of calling God *Yahweh*, but instructed me that the king of the north and the king of the south were only desert warlords contemporary with Daniel. I can still remember that early doubt insinuated by Oxy Armour, son of Armour of Ballymoney – was the king of the north not really Russia? was Daniel not prophecy at all but mere history? were the ten toes of Nebuchadnezzar's statue just ten toes? – as in some ways more traumatic than later, more substantial doubts about the last day, heaven, hell and my supposedly immortal soul.

When all is said and done, the Holy Scriptures remain. 'Train up a child in the way he should go and when he is old it will not depart from him.' So some of the more learned brethren used to gloss the familiar text 'Train up a child in the way he should go: and when he is old, he will not depart from it' (Proverbs 22:6) in order to explain how Scripture could be true even when errant children from privileged homes had all too obviously departed from the way in which they should have gone. The world might take the children away from the Holy Scriptures but could not take the Scriptures away from the children. So I count myself lucky that having departed from the Scriptures they have not departed from me.

'The grass withereth and the flower thereof falleth away: But the word of the Lord endureth forever' (1 Peter 1:24–5). 'Forever' is a long time in politics, but at least familiar words from forty years ago still mutter away in my head: Hebrews chapter 11, called by the brethren 'God's great roll call of faith'. 'And what shall I more say? for the time would fail me to tell of Gedeon, and of Barak, and of Samson, and of Jephthae; of David also, and Samuel, and of the prophets: Who through faith subdued kingdoms, wrought righteousness, obtained promises, stopped the mouths of lions, quenched the violence of fire, escaped the edge of the sword, out of weakness were made strong, waxed valiant in fight, turned to flight the armies of the aliens.' Or chapter 2 of the Epistle to the Philippians: 'Let this mind be in you, which was also in Christ Jesus: Who, being in the form of God, thought it not robbery to be equal with God: But made himself of no reputation, and took upon him the form of a servant, and was made in the likeness of men: And being found in fashion as a man, he humbled himself, and became obedient unto death, even the death of the cross. Wherefore God also hath highly exalted him, and given him a name which is above every name: That at the name of Jesus every knee should bow, of things in heaven, and things in earth, and things under the earth; And that every tongue should confess that Jesus Christ is Lord, to the glory of God the Father.'

Or, best of all, from chapter 8 of the Epistle to the Romans: 'What shall we then say to these things? If God be for us, who can be against us? He that spared not his own Son, but delivered him up for us all, how shall he not with him also freely give us all things? Who shall lay any thing to the charge of God's elect? It is God that justifieth. Who is he that condemneth? It is Christ that died, yea rather, that is risen again, who is even at the right hand of God, who also maketh intercession for us. Who shall separate us from the love of Christ? shall tribulation, or distress, or persecution, or famine, or nakedness, or peril, or sword?... Nay, in all these things we are more than conquerors through him that loved us. For I am persuaded, that neither death, nor life, nor angels, nor principalities, nor powers, nor things present, nor things to come, nor height, nor depth, nor any other creature, shall be able to separate us from the love of God, which is in Christ Jesus our Lord.'

What it all means is something of a question, but that it is very beautiful and something of a comfort is without question. An old preacher of my youth was fond of reading and preaching from Ruth's plea to Naomi: 'Intreat me not to leave thee, or to return from following after thee: for whither thou goest, I will go; and where thou lodgest, I will lodge: thy people shall be my people, and thy God my God: Where thou diest, will I die, and there will I be buried: the Lord do so to me, and more also, if ought but death part thee and me' (Ruth 1: 16–17). Having read this text he would never fail to remark, 'There's nothing finer in the whole of literature,' always adding, quite inconsequentially, 'and I'm no authority, for I haven't got the qualifications.'

A deeply ingrained knowledge of the Scriptures is surely one happy outcome, one privilege, as the brethren would have it, of having been brought up by those peculiar people. It is hard to think of any other, unless it be an equally deep-rooted pessimism about worldly endeavour. Of course the brethren are eschatological, pearly-gate optimists, but they would never aspire to build the New Jerusalem in England's or any other green and pleasant land. There is indeed a happy land, but it is far, far away. And far, far away is surely the right place for the happy land. 'For here we have no continuing city, but we seek one to come' (Hebrews 13:14).

> I'm but a stranger here,
> Heaven is my home.
> Earth is a desert drear,
> Heaven is my home.
> Danger and sorrow stand
> Round me on every hand,
> Heaven is my fatherland,
> Heaven is my home.

As the late Sir Basil Brooke (as he was then styled) complained many years ago: Peculiar people, those Plymouth Brethren; they don't vote.

> Only one life, it will soon be past,
> Only what's done for Jesus will last.

Or, as I should now prefer to say,

Only one life, it will soon be past,
Not even what's done for Jesus will last.

Better still, as the Preacher himself, the son of David, puts it: 'What profit hath a man of all his labour which he taketh under the sun? One generation passeth away, and another generation cometh: but the earth abideth forever. The sun also ariseth and the sun goeth down, and hasteth to the place where he arose. The wind goeth toward the south, and turneth about unto the north; it whirleth about continually, and the wind returneth again according to his circuits. All the rivers run into the sea; yet the sea is not full ... All things are full of labour; man cannot utter it ... There is no remembrance of former things; neither shall there be any remembrance of things that are to come with those that shall come after' (Ecclesiastes 1:3–11).

'He was in the world, and the world was made by him, and the world knew him not' (John 1:10). If the world did not know Christ, then we preferred to know nothing of the world, or so at least we said. So then, even as the world had rejected Christ, we would reject the world, that desert drear 'with all its pomp and show'. 'On terms of what almost may be called negation', writes Gosse, remembering the ways of the brethren in the middle of the nineteenth century. Looking back on the brethren of the early twentieth century, I too am struck, and on wet summer Sunday evenings saddened, by all the negation of my own youth. Ridiculous, that waste sad time:

Pulpits and sundayes, sorrow dogging sinne.

What did the brethren actually do? Certainly, when a young man or a young woman got saved the brethren expected that there would be signs following. If any man is in Christ Jesus he is a new creature, or a new creation, as those with Greek liked to gloss it. For all that they are sometimes accused of overvaluing faith at the expense of works ('For by grace are ye saved through faith; and that *not of yourselves*: it is the gift of God', Ephesians 2:8), I think it is fairer to say that while the brethren surely believed that works without faith were valueless – mere righteousness, they were forever reminding themselves, was like filthy rags (Isaiah 64:6) – they did not have a wholly Lutheran contempt for the Epistle of James, accepting that faith without works is dead, that is, nonexistent. It is here that their negativity

97

comes in, for it must be admitted that the brethren had a very negative view of the works which were to be the outer criterion of an inner process. Not for them what Gosse calls the 'propaganda of beneficence, the constant attention to the moral and physical improvement of persons who have been neglected'.

Gosse is interesting about this. He points out that at the time when he was writing (1907) the revolution which had overturned the puritanism of which his father was he alleges 'perhaps the latest surviving type' had been so complete that now 'all classes of religious persons combine in placing philanthropic activity, the objective attitude, in the foreground ... so that nowadays a religion which does not combine with its subjective faith a strenuous labour for the good of others is hardly held to possess any religious principle worth proclaiming'. However, as Gosse goes on to argue, the propaganda of beneficence is a relatively recent accretion to Christianity and does not loom large in the writings of seventeenth-century divines. Jeremy Taylor would not have thought that 'any activity of the district-visitor or the Salvation lassie came within the category of saintliness'.

The brethren whom I knew would have agreed with Philip Gosse and Jeremy Taylor. They were obsessively subjective, their aspirations being, as Gosse has it, 'individual and metaphysical' rather than philanthropic. The only district-visiting they did was with gospel tracts. It is true that they greatly admired doctors who brought modern drugs and surgery to that part of central Africa which the brethren of my day called the Copperbelt, the fief it seemed of Ulster evangelicals. We would say 'medical missionary' in the sort of respectful tone of voice which the world might reserve for 'brain surgeon'. But the drugs and the surgery were supplementary to the main business of evangelism, springes to catch woodcock. Many were the stories of the black man who had been led to Christ following a successful appendectomy.

Patricia Beer remembers how a favourite poem of her youth was once the occasion of some theological controversy. It was Leigh Hunt's 'Abou Ben Adhem'. It will be remembered that Ben Adhem's name was not found written in the angel's book of the names of those who love the Lord. When he requested that his name be entered as one who loved his fellow men, not only was it done, but 'Lo! Ben Adhem's name led all the rest.' Not a brethren poem. As Mrs Beer points out, 'this was the most heinous heresy, as only the saving blood of Jesus could get anyone's name on any list that counted'. She adds that 'to the Plymouth Brethren love of one's fellow men was in itself suspect' which may, or may not, be going a bit far.

The young believer supplied evidence of the truth that was in him much more by what he did not do than by what he did, by what he was prepared to give up, i.e., worldly pleasures. If his abstentions were to be given a more positive look they might be described as renunciations, but that is as grammatical rather than a real positive. 'I have given up all for Jesus, this vain world means nought to me' the brethren would sing with a sort of dolorous self-congratulation. 'Earth's joys no longer charm me and the world has lost its hold.' Or:

My Jesus I love Thee, I know Thou art mine,
For Thee all the pleasures of sin I resign.

However, here was another difficulty. The great majority of our conversions were inside jobs: conversions of the children of the brethren themselves, and that nearly always at a tender age. Clearly it was difficult in such a case for the neophyte to demonstrate, by his disengagement from this vain world and his resignation from a round of sinful pleasures, much in the way of a changed life. Old things might, indeed old things must have passed away, all things being now new (2 Corinthians 5:17) but to the outward eye it must have seemed very much like business as usual. When, aged thirteen, I got saved for the last time, I neither smoked nor drank, nor did I commit fornication and I had never been inside a cinema. What then could I give up for Jesus? Cricket? Or perhaps the *Hotspur* and the *Wizard* or William and Biggles for whom in the alien environment of boarding school I had developed a furtive passion that reflected little credit on my upbringing in a Christian home.

I remember one pimply boy relating the story of his conversion (a willingness to give one's testimony, as this exercise was called, being itself something of an indicator of the new life) who, having stumbled his way through the clichés obligatory to the occasion – I went to bed that night but not to sleep for I realised that I was a guilty hell-deserving sinner and that if I died as indeed I might that very night I would go straight to hell and the Lake of Fire for all eternity – then supplied as an example of the past enormities that had brought him to such an extremity the confession that he has been wont on winter evenings, in the company of his unsaved young companions, to knock on the doors of strangers and run away. I never once heard a newly saved adolescent (and I have heard many of them, including, in memory's embarrassed ear, myself) confess to an unregenerate taste for masturbation which the Lord Jesus Christ was giving him the strength to give up. Such a one's mother, sitting proudly for the first time, as she might have put it, under young Alexander's ministry, would have had a fit.

In a short time our young preacher will learn that there is no real need to be too explicit about his sins, past or present. Like Mark Rutherford's acquaintance Holderness, the travelling draper, he will 'confess crimes which, to say the truth, although they are many according to his own account, are never given in that detail which would make his confession of some value. He will never pray without telling all of us that there is no health in him, and that his soul is a mass of putrefying sores; but everyone will think the better of him for his self-humiliation.'

If conversions from outside the brethren community were rare then the conversion of a grown-up son or daughter from a brethren family who had escaped unsaved into his or her twenties was in my experience even rarer. He, more often than she, daughters being more tractable and therefore likely to be garnered young, was sometimes to be seen, especially in country districts, attending out of respect for his pious old mother the special gospel meetings held during the late summer in a large canvas tent pitched in a corner of one of his father's fields, a mood-matching location for so many bleak jeremiads: 'The harvest is past, the summer is ended, and we are not saved' (8:20). I can see him now, twenty-seven years old, large, awkward and innocent, sitting between his aged parents, well to the front of the rustic congregation. The visiting evangelist, a long-time friend of the old folk, knows very well how his stock will go up through the length and breadth of Ulster if he can net this one, the only unsaved child of a prosperous County Armagh farmer. In imagination he can already hear himself recollecting the devoutly-to-be-wished consummation: 'Yes indeed we had a good six weeks just outside Loughgall last August and September. Night after night the Lord Himself was present in a very real way and gave blessing. Ten professed to be saved, including young Samuel Mawhinney, that's right, Sam's boy. You should have seen old Sarah. Aaaagh, overjoyed she was, she could hardly speak, with the big, big tears running down her cheeks.'

Now, however, young Samuel has to endure much personal

reference and allusion, which just stops short of naming him as the wandering sheep this shepherd is after. The opening hymn is given out:

> There are loved ones in the glory
> Whose dear forms we oft-times miss.
> When you close your earthly story,
> Will you join them in their bliss?
> Will the circle be unbroken by and by
> In a better world that's waiting in the sky?

and his mother can hardly get through it unaffected. In the opening prayer there will be the familiar reference to those who have been the 'children of many prayers' i.e., those children of brethren families who have had the advantage of being much prayed for – prayed for, as the preacher in such a context never fails to remark, 'even before they were born'. Then a second hymn will be given out.

> There were ninety and nine that safely lay,
> In the shelter of the fold.
> But one was out in the hills away,
> Far off from the gates of gold.
> Out in the mountains wild and bare,
> Away from the tender shepherd's care.

Before we sing, the evangelist preaches a bit from the original (Luke 15:3–7) tending to slide over both the gospel truth that the sheep were abandoned in the wilderness and not in Sankey's sentimental fold, and the sarcastic reference to the ninety and nine just persons who needed no repentance. There are indeed ninety-nine (well, ninety-five) just, or, it would be better to say justified persons in the tent, but they are not smug, unrepentant Pharisees; they are simple sinners who in their day and generation have appreciated the necessity of repentance and have as a consequence been saved by grace. But what the preacher really wants to emphasise is not irrelevant subtleties like these but only

Samuel's minority status, which he will surely want to change, together with the rejoicing there will be in heaven tonight to say nothing of the happiness at his mother's supper table if one, just one wanderer is found.

And all through the mountain, thunder riven,
And up from the rocky steep,
There arose a cry to the gates of Heaven:
Rejoice, I have found my sheep.
And the angels echoed around the throne,
Rejoice for the Lord brings back His own!

The text for the address will be taken aptly enough from the story of the prodigal son as related in chapter 15 of Luke's Gospel, the story of a farmer's boy who was lost and then found: 'I will arise and go to my father, and will say unto him Father, I have sinned against heaven and before thee and am no more worthy to be called thy son; make me as one of thy hired servants … But when he was yet a great way off, his father saw him and had compassion, and ran, and fell on his neck, and kissed him.' What rejoicing there would be should some prodigal this very evening, tired of a life of sin and debauchery and riotous living in a far country, repent of his sins and return to a loving Father who is ready and willing, nay who is longing to forgive him.

They brought forth the robe and the ring,
Made merry, did dance and did sing,
Did dance and did laugh
Round the fatted calf,
While the father himself he did sing:
Glory to God he's come home!
From guilt and from crime
And from feeding the swine,
Glory to God he's come home!

Samuel's life of course bears little resemblance to the story of the boy in the parable, except perhaps in the matter of feeding the swine. He works a twelve-hour day in his father's fields and has never been tempted to be prodigal. The nearest he has come to riotous living in a far country was his last holiday two years ago when, to his mother's manifest distress, he spent a week in Blackpool ('to see the lights') with the Young Farmers, Presbyterian or Church of Ireland to a man, three young lady farmers, also unsaved, being of the party.

A complementary sub-plot also having to do with fathers and returning sons introduces into the story a text from Genesis (44:34). Here is an example of the great facility with which the brethren used texts from the Old Testament which had no obvious reference to the gospel message but which were adaptable. Some brethren indeed claimed that the gospel was implicit in every verse of both Testaments. My father, who was far from sceptical, doubted this, and asked one such how he would preach the gospel from 'He saith among the trumpets, Ha, Ha ...' (Job 39:25) or from 1 Chronicles 26:18, which reads in its entirety 'At Parbar westward, four at the causeway, and two at Parbar.' His interlocutor alleged that the passage from Job far from being irrelevant had been instrumental in the salvation of a racing man who had realised after a succession of losers that even the horses were laughing at him. He conceded however that the verse from Chronicles allocating the divisions of the porters among the sons of Kore and Merari had no obvious application. Happily, our text is not so arcane, being taken from the story of Joseph's conspiracy to keep Benjamin in Egypt, having for that purpose framed his youngest brother by planting apparently stolen goods in his baggage. The older brothers are alarmed, for Jacob has parted with the favourite, Benjamin, only with the greatest reluctance and will surely die if he is detained. And so in our text Judah pleads with Joseph, 'For how shall I go up to my father, and the lad be not with me?' Judah's words are of course the perfect epitome of Sarah's thoughts. How can she go up to her Father (in heaven) if Samuel is not coming too? Surely

104

the lad must see the point and get saved if only to please his old mother.

And now the preacher gives out the closing hymn, reading slowly, with a great show of solemnity, the opening verse:

Almost persuaded, now to believe,
Almost persuaded, Christ to receive,
Seems now some soul to say,
Go, Spirit, go Thy way,
Some more convenient day
On Thee I'll call.

'We recall,' he goes on, 'how it is related in the book of the Acts of the Apostles that those very important men, the king, Agrippa, and the governor, Felix, were privileged to sit under the ministry of the great apostle himself, and when King Agrippa was warned by that faithful servant of Christ of the judgment to come we read that his response was: "Almost thou persuadest me to be a Christian." And the apostle replied, "would that thou wert both almost and altogether as I am except these bonds". Sinner friend in our little meeting this evening, let me tell you kindly but solemnly, as one who is burdened with a great care for your immortal soul, for your eternal welfare, that the distance between altogether and almost is the distance between eternal weal and eternal woe. It is the distance between heaven and hell.

Almost persuaded, harvest is past,
Almost persuaded, doom comes at last.
'Almost' can not avail,
'Almost' is but to fail,
Sad, sad the bitter wail;
'Almost, but lost!'

'And what of the governor, what of Felix? We read that he came with his wife Drusilla to hear Paul reasoning concerning the faith in Christ. What a privilege! When we think of our poor stammering words in the gospel this evening and compare them with the eloquence of the great apostle to the Gentiles! And as Paul reasoned of righteousness, temperance and the judgment to come we read that Felix trembled. Ay! and doubtless there are those in our meeting tonight who are also privileged, the children perhaps of many prayers, prayed for even before you were born, sung to sleep with the songs of Zion, who, like Timothy, have from a child known the Holy Scriptures which are able to make thee wise unto salvation, and you have trembled in the past and you tremble again tonight. But sinner friend, let me tell you this: trembling never got one single, solitary sinner into heaven. Of Felix, we read that although he trembled, he said to Paul, "Go thy way for this time; when I have a convenient season I will call for thee." But as we read in the Second Epistle of Paul to the Corinthians chapter 6 and verse 2, it is *now* that is the accepted time, *now* is the day of salvation. Unhappy Felix [this without the smallest hint of a smile – the evangelist is not joking], Holy Scripture records of him only that willing to show the Jews a favour he left Paul bound, never that he found that convenient season. Alas! Poor Felix!

Alas! Poor Samuel!* As one of Graham Greene's thoughtful policemen says, poor all of us when you come to think of it. Outside in the damp, indigo gloaming, loose heifers nudge against the walls of the tent, and the clouds return after the rain.

Mature conversions, whether of the children of many prayers or of rank, unprayed-for outsiders were, although – or because – rare, greatly prized, yielding as they did better evidence of a changed life than could be got from a fifteen-year-old's

*[Samuel Mawhinney was saved at special gospel meetings conducted by my late father and the late Mr Moses Bartholomew in the Gospel Hall, The Mall, Armagh, in 1956. A quiet, consistent brother, he was a pillar of the local assembly until his homecall in 1985 at the age of sixty-two – *F.S.A.S.*]

autobiography. Not that even these extramural pasts were ever really spectacular. From time to time we might hear from a reformed drunkard, or at least a reformed drinker, but never from a thief or an adulterer or even a fornicator. A much more typical subject for admiring comment would be the young woman who had forsworn the cinema ('the silver screen'), or cosmetics ('make-up'), or dancing ('the dance floor'), or the young man who had given up football matches ('Every Saturday afternoon would have seen me on the terraces at Window Park or following Linfield to away matches') or the public house or cigarettes ('I used to be a forty-a-day man').

This last was something of a test case and on one occasion the trigger of a moderately successful pun by a frivolous young brother, not well received by his elders for whom the words of Holy Writ were no joking matter. Brethren were apt to refer to their past unregenerate lives, as indeed to much else, in highly colourful language from the Old Testament. Thus they might recall the hole of the pit from which they were digged (Isaiah 51:1) or describe themselves as being brands plucked from the burning (Zechariah 3:2).

> He plucked me from the jaws of Hell,
> My Jesus has done all things well.

So, when it happened that a recently converted young man had been seen in a public place with a cigarette in his mouth, he was not unnaturally the subject of adverse comment. Ought he not to be rebuked by the elder brethren? Inspired, the frivolous brother proposed that the backslider would appear to be a brand plucked from the burning and still smoking.

The cinema was something to be given up smartly, a paradigm of sin, and no saved person would darken the door of what some of the older folk still called a picture palace. I remember, in 1947, my mother was more than somewhat shocked to learn that one of her female cousins, together with a party of Belfast sisters, had, anonymous in London, under the brown fog of a winter afternoon, sneaked into a cinema to see the newsreel of the wedding of Her Royal Highness the Princess Elizabeth and Lieutenant Philip Mountbatten RN. True, they had tried to time their visit so as to see nothing but the newsreel, though in consequence of over-prudential punctuality they had been subjected to the last five minutes (but only the last five minutes) of the main feature – 'And why anyone should want to see *that* sort of thing ... ?' they sighed. True, again, Windsorphilia was quite properly mitigating. Nevertheless, I imagine my mother thought that the excursion was, along with wars and rumours of wars, a sign that we had indeed entered upon the last days.

The attitude of the brethren was understandable, the cinema being, in those days before television, the most popular of godless, lower-middle-class, worldly pleasures and so conspicuously to be avoided by the lower-middle-class, unwordly brethren. The pictures were, as everyone knew, immoral fantasies acted out by lascivious actors and actresses, a potent source of temptation for our young people. To remember the typical plot of a Hollywood film in the 1930s and 1940s is to find at least part of this judgement eccentric, though perhaps the brethren were more percipient about the lives of actors and actresses than was the average filmgoer of the time. Now I imagine most of the brethren have television sets on which, out of the eye of the world, they may or may not watch films which in 1940 would have been beyond the dreams of concupiscence. What will they make of an ordinary commercial film I saw recently in which the former mistress of the murdered hero in a fond gesture of farewell hikes up her skirt, masturbates and smears her vaginal juices around the nostrils of the corpse? Will they be as shocked as the decent, godless, hell-bound one-and-nines in 1938 would surely have been?

It should be remembered that to many conservatives in our assemblies all fictions were immoral, though sentimental women like my mother were addicted to the stories of Annie S. Swan, Amy Le Feuvre, Gene Stratton Porter and Louisa M. Alcott, to the multi-volume saga of Elsie Dinsmore, to *Pixie O'Shaugnessy* by Mrs G. De Horne Vaizey, to Mrs O. F. Walton, author of *A Peep Behind the Scenes* and (to the pure all things are pure) *Christie's Old Organ*. An evangelist of our acquaintance, composed of sterner stuff, made the headlines of his local paper, the *Ardglass Bugle*, after a sermon, the gravamen of which was that all novelists are in hell, the evidence cited being Revelation 22:15: 'For without are dogs, and sorcerers, and whoremongers, and murderers, and idolaters, and whosoever loveth and maketh a lie.' Poor Mrs O. F. Walton: the company she kept! My mother would certainly have flinched from such a vigorous deduction, like the young Edmund Gosse on hearing that his beloved Shakespeare was now a lost soul suffering for his sins in hell, though I fear she would have been more concerned about Mrs Swan's eternal destiny than about that of Shakespeare. Yet the conclusion was worrying, for did not these treble-barrelled American ladies at least love to make up stories, and were not 'You're making it up' and 'You're telling stories' practically synonyms for 'You're lying'?

In Bangor, County Down, in the 1930s, we lived only half a mile away from the Tonic cinema, a pleasure dome entirely of its time, large by any standards and huge in provincial Bangor, the most sumptuous building in town. I passed it every day on my way to school, never failing to stop and examine the posters and the still photographs, drawn by the dreadful mystery of the place. My school friends talked excitedly about Gene Autry and Roy Rogers and Bud Abbott and Lou Costello but I realised that it could not be for me. Although I was seven years old and unsaved, and therefore bound for the same hell as the Saturday morning film fans, if not, as the privileged child of many prayers, for one a great deal hotter, I knew better than to advance sophistically my worldling status as a reason for indulging in worldly practice. I recognised that it was my parents' duty to keep me unspotted from the world (James 1:27). As they were fond of remarking, you did not taste poison in order to test the strength. So I sighed as a potential lover and consented as a dutiful son.

When I was thirteen years old I was offered my first serious opportunity to go to the cinema. By this time I believed myself to be saved, at least during the weeks when I was not tormented by doubts that I had failed to believe properly in Jesus Christ. At any given moment then I would either have considered myself saved or at least been desirous of being saved, and during the weeks I believed myself to be saved I was not as yet half ashamed of that condition, but in a priggish way rather proud to be out of the broad way and on to the narrow path, *au fait* with the New Testament scheme of things, a mystery not revealed to many. I was by then a boarder at Cabin Hill Preparatory School, and so out of my mother's immediate jurisdiction. As Gosse says, 'Little boys from quiet, pious households, commonly found, in those days, a chasm yawning at the feet of their inexperience when they arrived at Boarding-school.' So it was with me, on the 8th of May 1945, VE Day, when the school was given a whole holiday, the boarders to be taken into the city in the afternoon to see *Five Minutes* (or was it Five Seconds?) *Over Tokyo*. The chasm yawned as Satan tempted me, but I passed the test, nailing my colours to the mast as the brethren liked to say, and declined the treat, because 'as a Christian I did not go to the cinema'. It was not, I insisted, that I had been forbidden by my mother to do so but rather that as a Christian I really had lost any desire for such things. The world, as I explained to the headmaster, had lost its hold. The younger masters sneered openly, recognising lower-class, mission-hall Protestantism when they saw it, whereas the other boys, less worldly-wise, merely thought me rather eccentric or perhaps peculiar. So I spent that cloudless spring afternoon, solitary in the Lake Field, smugly practising the high jump, on one occasion lifting myself a well-deserved 4 feet 3 inches nearer heaven.

Some years later there was another opportunity to see inside some Astoria or Coliseum. By now I was much less happy about my unique (at least at Campbell College) born-again status. I was becoming increasingly self-conscious about my divided life, the greater part of it spent at school in the east of Belfast, holidays and most Sundays spent at home with my mother on the Stranmillis Road. The Sundays were frequent because my mother had put pressure on my housemaster, on compassionate grounds that she was a widow and crippled and that I was her only child, for exeats far beyond the norm. On these Sundays I was willy-nilly involved in gospel hall activities which, though I still half believed in them, I was glad were unwitnessed by more sophisticated eyes – teaching a Sunday school class, knocking on doors distributing gospel tracts. ('We've tracked the whole of New-townbreda,' remarked one perspiring brother on a hot, hot day in July, and I felt like a junior hound of heaven.)

Of these exercises one of the most embarrassing was a march from the gospel hall around the neighbouring streets to advertise the about-to-begin gospel meeting. Three abreast, at the

111

burnt-out end of a smoky November Sunday (at six o'clock) we would strike out, big Jim Sheridan at our head. At intervals *en route*, without breaking our step, Jim or some other brother, as the Lord led, would shout out an invitation to 'the sinner friends within the sound of my voice' together with the venue of the meeting, the name of the speaker and a word of Scripture, always of course citing chapter and verse. 'The Epistle of Paul to the Romans chapter one and verse sixteen, "For I am not ashamed of the gospel of Christ: for it is the power of God unto salvation to every one that believeth; to the Jew first, and also to the Greek."' And then we would all burst into song:

I'm not ashamed to own my Lord
Or to defend His cause.

But by now I *was* ashamed and very glad that the murk, together with the meanness of the vicinity, all but precluded any possibility of my being spotted, by a rich acquaintance from Campbell, in the company of such peculiar people.

Therefore when, in the interest of the furtherance of sixth-form geography, it was proposed that we should visit the local cinema to see a film about Australian graziers (*The Overlanders*, with Chips Rafferty), I was no longer disposed to make myself conspicuous. And so, at last, I passed through those ornate portals, past a painted Jezebel at the receipt of custom, up the carpeted stairs under the eyes of Alan Ladd, Lana Turner, Joan Crawford, Nigel Patrick, Anna Neagle, Richard Attenborough, Vivien Leigh, Jean Kent, Alastair Sim, David Niven, Cornel Wilde, Bette Davis, Dirk Bogarde and the rest, names and faces now, but not for much longer, unfamiliar to me, and into the dark, redolent of tobacco smoke and cheap scent, as different and as awful as a Roman Catholic church (not that I had ever been there either). In the blackness I sat perched high on what seemed to be the narrowest seat I had ever been seriously offered. After some minutes, noticing my predicament, my neighbour showed me how the seat tilted. A likable son of the manse from Letterkenny, he whispered, 'I don't often come to these places myself.'

And now I was hooked, a pictures addict, so made, perhaps, in the way that people have been said to become alcoholics through being deprived of sensible drinking *en famille*. Would a homoeopathic innoculation of *Snow White and the Seven Dwarfs* have given me the strength, like McConville of Letterkenny, to take it or leave it?

The Christmas holidays began and I went to work for the Post Office. Being an honest seventeen, indeed a Christian, I did my rounds efficiently, completing the second delivery before the lights came on at four. I went back to headquarters to clock off and leave my bag and torch with the old postman who was my minder and who was appalled by the efficiency. 'Ah, not at all, son,' he said. 'You're far too early.' He winked. 'You could never have got that great big bag of cards delivered that quick, so you couldn't. Away home and have your tea and come back about seven. Sure a wee bit of overtime never did anyone any harm, did it?'

The Ritz beckoned. And so I sneaked back into the dark to see *No Room at the Inn*, a film I was never to see again, with, as I discovered many years later, a screenplay by Dylan Thomas. The next furtive *cinq à sept* was spent at the Mayfair where I saw *The Third Man*, with Orson Welles and zither, and then, the following day, it was to the Hippodrome for *The Hasty Heart* with Richard Todd and Patricia Neal and the future leader of the free world.

Those places, as McConville referred to them, how pleasant they were forty years ago! From one o'clock to ten o'clock they always seemed comfortably full, not overcrowded, relaxed, with a constant coming and going. Nobody felt constrained to actually see any picture from the beginning; it often seemed all the more interesting back to front, like a shop girl's cardigan buttoned up the spine. 'This,' as we said in those days, in those places, 'is where we came in.'

Some months later, at university in Belfast, with its forty cinemas, I would skip lectures to see two and sometimes three double features every day. It might be the Astoria, Knock, at one o'clock (Susan Hayward and Dana Andrews in *My Foolish Heart*), then a quick run between suburbs to the Strand, Belmont, for the picture starting at four or thereabouts. Hours later I would emerge, blinking in the bright summer sunshine of early evening, amazed, dazzled at the contrast with the violence and mean streets of *G-Men*, so bewitched, bemused by the Chicago demotic of those hard men as to be thinking out of the side of my mouth (as Gilbert Ryle never quite said); then I would take a trolley bus into the city centre in time for the Imperial, Cornmarket, at half past seven, (Bob Hope and Jane Russell in *The Paleface*).

Dane Clark, Jeanne Crain, Evelyn Keyes, Dana Andrews, Margaret Lockwood, Linda Darnell, Michael Wilding, Anne Baxter, Van Heflin, Doris Day, Dennis Price, Bonar Colleano, Trevor Howard, Margaret Leighton, Ann Sheridan, Ruth Roman, Glenn Ford, Lana Morris, Joseph Cotten, Jennifer Jones, Maxwell Reed, Muriel Pavlow, Valerie Hobson, Robert Montgomery, James Hayter, Jane Wyman, Miles Malleson, John Gregson, Ann Miller, Beatrice Campbell, Fred MacMurray, Leo Genn, Natasha Parry, Cecil Parker, Paul Douglas, Stewart Granger, Robert Morley, Kay Walsh, Tony Curtis, Celia Johnson, Donna Reed, Gene Kelly, Rhonda Fleming, Eric Portman, Betsy Blair, Anna Neagle, Richard Widmark, Patricia Roc, Gene Tierney, Merle Oberon, Ray Milland, James Stewart, Richard Conte, Celeste Holm, James Cagney, George Sanders, Veronica Lake, Kenneth More, Robert Donat, Loretta Young, Arthur Kennedy, Marilyn Maxwell, Mercedes McCambridge, Cesar Romero, Diane Cilento, Kay Kendal, James Mason, Humphrey Bogart, Virginia Mayo, Kirk Douglas, Alida Valli, Van Johnson, Betty Grable, George Raft, Farley Granger, Peter Ustinov, Arlene Dahl, James

Robertson Justice, Cyd Charisse, Jean Gabin, Bernard Lee, André Morell, Dulcie Gray, Don Ameche, Spencer Tracy, Shelley Winters, Basil Radford, Brian Aherne, Simone Signoret, Broderick Crawford, Leslie Caron, Zachary Scott, Robert Newton, Joan Caulfield, Louis Calhern, Robert Mitchum, Jack Hawkins, Gary Merrill, Deborah Kerr, Yvonne de Carlo, Donald Houston, Dinah Sheridan, Anthony Steel, Myrna Loy, Jacques Tati, Debbie Reynolds, Michael Denison, June Allyson, Danny Kaye, Jeanne Moreau, Grace Kelly, Joan Greenwood, Cyril Cusack, Anita Ekberg, William Hartnell, Christine Norden, Robert Cummings, Kathleen Ryan, Teresa Wright, William Holden, Janette Scott, Alec Guinness, Elizabeth Taylor, Harry Fowler, Glynis Johns, William Bendix, Ida Lupino, Leslie Howard, MacDonald Carey, Lizabeth Scott, Ricardo Montalban, June Haver, Naunton Wayne, Sylvia Syms, Richard Greene, Ann Todd, Edwige Feuillere, Greer Garson, Louis Jourdan, Joan Fontaine, Randolph Scott, Thelma Ritter, Edmund Purdom, Lana Turner, David Farrar, Jean Kent, Claudette Colbert, Jack Warner, Olivia de Havilland, Kim Novak, Karl Malden, Katharine Hepburn, Jack Watling, Gloria Grahame, Dan Duryea, Helen Cherry, Rita Hayworth, Chips Rafferty, where are you now? Just reeling off your names is ever so comfy.

My long affair with the cinema was furtive on at least two levels. First, my exits from and entrances into those places were devious, with cap pulled down and handkerchief up, affecting an incipient sneeze, for fear of being spotted by passing saints. Second, I fairly soon became if not actually ashamed of, at least embarrassed by an addiction to a form of entertainment I thought unworthy of an intellectual. Would T. S. Eliot patronise three cinemas within the space of eight hours? I rather thought not. In *The Cocktail Party*, just then published, Eliot writes:

A common interest in the moving pictures
Frequently brings young people together.

True, the words are spoken by a character in the play, who is, I reminded myself, no more Eliot than Macbeth is Shakespeare. Nevertheless, it sounded a bit like Eliot and I could not help feeling that the master would be every bit as snooty as his creature.

The term 'cineaste' was not then in vogue, perhaps not even in the dictionary. Even if it had been, I doubt if I would have been any more impressed then by that sort of sophistication than I am now. There were, after all, even in those days, some who affected to discover a difference not merely of degree but of kind between foreign films and the products of Ealing and Hollywood. I thought *Bicycle Thieves* and *Les Enfants du Paradis* were just two more pictures, not improved by subtitling, and anyway not in the same class as *The Third Man* and *All About Eve*.

Worldly books rather than worldly films would, I decided, be the thing. Here was an escape from the brethren quite as beguiling as the pictures, but intellectually much more *comme il faut*. Laurence Olivier's Max de Winter was only nonsense out of Daphne du Maurier, but Herr Issyvoo was Christopher Isherwood. My identification could be complete and unashamed. Christopher was a failed student who was making himself a writer. Christopher was observant, Christopher was, just as I would have been, passionately in love with the beautiful, promiscuous extrovert Sally Bowles but, shy and introspective just like me, not very good at pressing his suit. Ah, the innocence of those early readings!

> Lay your sleeping head, my love,
> Human on my faithless arm.

If anyone had told me then that Auden was serenading a fellow and Isherwood was more interested in young Otto Nowak than in Sally, I would have been not so much appalled as incredulous.

Books were an escape too in quite another sense. Not only did they give me three hours with Scobie in Freetown, or with Aziz in Chandrapore or with Christopher in Berlin. 'From my window the deep, solemn massive street … I am a camera with its shutter open …' They suggested a simple way out of the whole brethren charade. I too could be a camera.

This desire to be a writer was first conceived, as is perhaps too readily the case, when I was in the upper sixth, reading English for the Higher Schools Certificate. Mr Felix Jones would rap out, whether as a constituent part of or as a diversion from his teaching never being entirely clear, modern bestsellers and *succès d'estime* whose titles had been culled from the works of Shakespeare.

Rose MacCauley *Told by an Idiot* – *Macbeth*
Christopher Isherwood *All the Conspirators* – *Julius Caesar*
Somerset Maugham *Cakes and Ale* – *Twelfth Night*
Aldous Huxley *Brave New World* – *The Tempest*
Nigel Balchin *A Sort of Traitors* – *Richard II*
J. B. Priestley *Bright Day* – *Julius Caesar*

It is the bright day, he would continue, that brings forth the adder, thus communicating an agreeable frisson to three bookish youngsters, McCaughey, Simmons and myself, the English sixth form.

These titles, enigmatic without a supplied context printed as epigraph on an inside page, and often mysterious enough with it, as in Isherwood's novel or, as we moved on:

Aldous Huxley *Antic Hay* – *Edward II* (Marlowe)

seemed to us the height of sophistication. We looked for our own examples. I found in the school fiction library a thriller by a now hardly remembered writer, remembered by me only for his Shakespearian borrowing:

Sidney Horler *Cue for Passion* – *Hamlet*

This was judged not quite the thing, indeed so far from the thing as, if admitted to the canon, seriously to derogate from the achievements of better men. As to what was to count as 'better' men we were prepared to go as low as Howard Spring. *There is no Armour (Shirley), Fame is the Spur (Lycidas),* and *My Son! My Son!* (2 Samuel 18:33), but no lower.

Horler was then, we agreed, innocent of the intention we admired in Huxley and Maugham (no quotation appeared as epigraph on an inside page) and meant by *Cue for Passion* simply cue for passion, much as his better-known contemporary, James Hadley Chase, meant by *No Orchids for Miss Blandish* no orchids for Miss Blandish, no more, no less.

Simmons reported that his sister was reading a book called

We are for the Dark. Could this be a spoof of *Gentlemen Prefer Blondes?*

Author unknown   *We are for the Dark – Antony and Cleopatra*

This was, because quite funny, better than Horler, but in the absence of further research, only hearsay. It was unsatisfactory too in that, being funny, it detracted from the high seriousness which we were sure should always attend the art of the making of titles of books.

We longed to emulate these masters and soon became prolific writers of titles. Donne's sermons and devotions were surely a mine of which every rift would be loaded with recoverable ore, rich seams having been already suggested by Hemingway's famous find and by Nigel Balchin's less well-known, but to our mind superior exercise in the genre. To Balchin we awarded the palm; he was the master against whose high standards we would measure our own efforts.

> There have been many examples of men, that have bin their owne executioneres, and that have made hard shift to bee so; some have always had poyson about them, in a hollow ring upon their finger, and some in their pen that they used to write with; some have beate out their braines at the wal of the prison, and some have eate the fire out of their chimneys; one is said to have come nearer to our case than so, to have strangled himself, though his hands were bound by crushing his throate between his knees; but I do nothing upon myself and yet am MINE OWNE EXECUTIONER.

We researched these devotions and sermons thoroughly, if only through the pages of the Nonesuch edition, but alas could turn up nothing comparable to the exciting discoveries of Hemingway and Balchin. McCaughey proposed *Somewhat a Strange Topique*, spelling, to be sure, *sic.* 'And there may be examples of women that have thought it a fit way to gain a soul by prostituting themselves and by entertaining unlawful love with a purpose to entertain a servant, which is somewhat a strange topique to

119

draw arguments of religion from.' This had at least the advantage of setting us up in the Graham Greene business of drawing arguments of religion from a strange topic (sex). My suggestion, *Methuselah's Half-holiday*, was weaker still and had no such advantage. 'What a dimme vespers of a glorious festivall, what a poore half-holidaye, is Methusalem's nine hundred years to eternity.' It might just about do to impress the brethren with my learning in some future sermon.

When we've been there ten thousand years,
Bright shining as the sun,
We've no less days to sing God's praise
Than when we first begun.

'Beloved brethren, when we contemplate an eternity to be spent in the presence of our beloved Lord, we cannot but help recalling the words of a seventeenth-century Dean of St Paul's Cathedral, the great metaphysical poet John Donne, who, many years ago, put it so beautifully when he wrote that compared with eternity even the nine hundred and sixty-nine years of the patriarch Methuselah's long life down here below were nothing but a poor half-holiday.' One in the eye for Dr Donaldson, the Inspector of Schools, who was in his Sunday morning homilies much given to reciting the more banal lines from Shakespeare – 'the quality of mercy is not strained', 'the devil can cite Scripture for his purpose', 'that bourn from which no traveller returns', 'a rose by any other name would smell as sweet' and so on. This last he would often quote in tandem with Matthew 1 and 21 – ' ... thou shalt call his name JESUS: for he shall save his people from their sins', arguing somewhat obscurely that while a rose might be called an onion and still be a rose, Jesus would not have been Jesus if he had not been 'Jesus'.

Could it be that the best titles were serendipitous? This comfortable hypothesis, which would obviate the chore of actually having to read sermons and devotions, shortly received confirmation, thus reinforcing a growing, soon to become chronic, idleness. There before my eyes, in scene 3 of act 2 of *Macbeth* lay a title as ingenious as any conceived by the great Balchin. 'Knock, knock, Who's there, i' the other devil's name? Faith, here's an equivocator that could swear in both scales against either scale, who committed treason enough for God's sake, yet could not equivocate to heaven. Oh come in, equivocator.' My book would be called:

Come in, Equivocator

Or, perhaps do you think, *Oh, Come in, Equivocator?* No, simply *Come in, Equivocator*. Perfection.

This title had the further merit that it suggested a work which would match Balchin not only in its excellence *qua* title. What Balchin had done for an alienist, exposing and connecting his private and his professional perplexities, I would do for a lawyer. Looking back, I am astounded at the euphoria generated by all this titlemaking. I was seventeen years old and, if not spectacularly ignorant, far from precociously knowledgeable. I might just, given a favourable wind from the south, have been able to tell a barrister from a solicitor. Yet I thought I was prepared, not indeed today, but tomorrow or next week or the week after or when, like Felix out of the book of the Acts of the Apostles, I found *A Convenient Season* (What do you think?), to write a book which would evince an easy familiarity with the minutiae of a lawyer's life.

These projects were of course never brought to the test, as other titles rushed in to usurp the position formerly held by *Come in, Equivocator*. By the following week, at the very outside, the best, the only title for a work of fiction would be:

Lords and Owners

This might to the superficial ear of the day have sounded like the latest novel by Miss Ivy Compton-Burnett. However, her couples, like Melchisidec, King of Salem, lacked pedigree, unlike mine. Look at the inside page.

They that have power to hurt, and will do none

121

That do not do the thing they most do show,
Who, moving others, are themselves as stone,
Unmoved, cold, and to temptation slow:
They rightly do inherit heaven's graces,
And husband nature's riches from expense,
These are the lords and owners of their faces
Others but stewards of their excellence.

What would be the theme of such a cleverly named work? It would chart the conflict between representatives of that class of persons who were, well, the lords and owners of their faces and that very different, but somehow complementary class of persons who were, well again, merely the stewards of their excellence. What else?

At one time I suggested that we need not restrict ourselves to Shakespeare and Donne, that excellent titles might, like books in the running brooks, be discovered in the most unlikely places. For example, I said, when I was mixed up with the Plymouth Brethren (falsely insinuating that those days were now a distant joke) we used to sing:

I am travelling on the Hallelujah Line
On the good old gospel train.

So, what about

The Hallelujah Line?

My fellow authors looked at me as if reason had quit its throne and I never again proposed anything so foolish. I did, however, recollecting my father's adversion to obscure passages of Scripture which were, he alleged, gospel-free, recommend to them Job 39 and 25: 'He saith among the trumpets, Ha, Ha: and he smelleth the battle afar off, the thunder of the captains, and the shouting.'

Ha! Ha! Among the Trumpets

This was much admired, but we did not realise that it had already been appropriated by Alun Lewis, himself already dead.

It was McCaughey who delivered the title to end all titles.

Modo and Mahu

'The Prince of Darkness is a gentleman, Modo, he's called, and Mahu' (*King Lear*).

We had to concede that it fairly took our breath away, and it has stayed with me through all the bookless decades between then and now both as *the* title for the book I will never write and as a sort of symbol for dead aspirations. What it meant then or means now, beyond just that, who knows? As Christopher Isherwood himself has said of *All the Conspirators*, it sounded grand. Or as we ourselves often said in those dear, dead days, shaking wise young heads over some conundrum, you might as well begin with the letters from Helen to her sister.*

* [A friend of mine who has some knowledge of these matters tells me that there is quite a lot of quotation and literary allusion scattered through this text. For example, when the author remarks of the film stars of the forties and fifties that 'just reeling off their names is ever so comfy', I am reliably informed that he is quoting the last line of 'Lakes', by the homosexual poet W. H. Auden (1907–73). In the reference above to Helen's letters I have been told that the author would seem to be referring to *Howards End*, a novel by the homosexual novelist E. M. Forster (1879–1970), which opens with the line: 'One might as well begin with the letters from Helen to her sister'. The author uses this sentence as if it were (I quote my knowledgeable friend) 'the idiomatic equivalent of such expressions as "You might as well talk to the door" or "You might as well go chasing after moonbeams", that is, "You might as well begin with the letters from Helen to her sister (for all the good it will do you)."' My friend informs me that this is of course not Forster's sense. Forster intends something like: 'Where shall we start? The letters from Helen to her sister would be as good a place as any.' There is no suggestion that the author was a homosexual. He leaves a wife and three daughters, all unsaved, for whom prayer is requested – *F.S.A.S.*]

In Edinburgh, when I was nineteen, my ambition to be a writer of something more than titles was further fanned when I discovered drink and public houses and took to it and them rather in the manner of a compulsive cinemagoer deprived in his youth of that entertainment. The forts of Rose Street – Milne's Bar, the Abbotsford, Paddy Crossan's – assumed the furniture of home, or, better still, a home from home.

> Faces along the bar
> Cling to their average day
> The lights must never go out
> The music must always play ...
> Lest we should see where we are,
> Lost in a haunted wood,
> Children afraid of the night,
> Who have never been happy or good.

It was in Rose Street that I first got to know some real poets, Norman MacCaig, Sidney Goodsir Smith ('Let me remain to my sad self hereafter, kind, comma, charitable, plonk' - that was genius, said Sidney) and the great Christopher Murray Grieve himself. Part of their charm for me, though it would have been the death of the acquaintance to breathe it, for their Anglophobia was profound, was that these kenspeckle persons seemed to be on first-name terms with writers in faraway London and New York who were actually well known: Dylan, Louis, Stephen, what Wystan said to Kit (!) Isherwood. Had I heard what Cyril had told an earnest young new statesman who had complained that he couldn't see how the Archbishop of Canterbury could reconcile being styled the father of the poor with his palaces and his huge salary? I had not heard. Cyril had replied that if the Archbishop couldn't answer a simple question like that he would still be a curate. Who was Cyril?

Cyril was Cyril Connolly and the next day I hurried up the Mound to the George IV bridge and the public library where I discovered *The Rock Pool, Enemies of Promise*, and, most exciting of all, *The Unquiet Grave*, finding the mix of romantic melancholy and nostalgic evocation of faraway places (Saint-Jean-de-Luz, Quai Bourbon, Rue de Vaugirard, Toulon, Almunecar, Ramatuelle, Sainte-Flour, Saint-Chely-d'Apcher, Velay, Vivarais, the Margeride, the Gerbier de Jonc, *Fitzroy Square, Charlotte Street, Chelsea*) irresistible. It was with some enthusiasm that I embraced the concept of angst, which seemed to have been made for me: 'remorse about the past, guilt about the present, anxiety about the future'. You could say that again! 'A frequent cause of angst is an awareness of the waste of our time and ability, such as may be witnessed among people kept waiting by a hairdresser.' How true!

'Today,' wrote Connolly, 'my deepest wish is to go to sleep for six months, if not for ever.' This was a novel thought, but a welcome one, especially in the six-month option. If Connolly, approaching forty, said he was about to heave his carcass of vanity, boredom and guilt into another decade, I, approaching twenty, felt very much the same and was not unpleased by my precocity.

'Both my happiness and unhappiness I owe to the love of pleasure; of sex, travel, reading, conversation (hearing oneself talk), food, drink, cigars and lying in warm water.' Clearly I had still my way to make in the world of worldly pleasure, in the *terra incognita* beyond reading, warm baths, and the cinema, whose absence from Connolly's list seemed only to confirm my suspicion that this worldly pleasure was insufficiently worldly.

Nevertheless, it was a comfort to know so well in advance that at the end of it all lay only more barbershop angst, already so keenly and so often experienced at the end of a day spent in three picture houses. Not so different, this angst, when you came to think of it, from the experience so often attested to by the newly saved sinner.

I tried the broken cisterns, Lord,
But, Ah the waters failed,
Even as I stooped to drink, they fled,
And mocked me as I wailed.
Now none but Christ can satisfy,
None other Name for me.
There's love and life and lasting joy
Lord Jesus found in Thee.

Except that now I knew better than the saved sinner. Salvation lay, Connolly had convinced me, not in Jesus Christ, but only in the production of a masterpiece. 'The more books we read, the clearer it becomes that the true function of a writer is to produce a masterpiece and that no other task is of any consequence.'

While he certainly worked on me as an *agent provocateur* of ambitious reverie (a masterpiece!), Connolly's real charm lay in his snapshots from what I took to be a writer's life, some so familiar that I seemed to live in them already ('first faint impressions of urban autumn'), some more remote, but a happy land not so far away as to be inaccessible.

August 7th: the first Autumn day. For once I have lived in the present! Walked to the book-shop at closing time. Raining. A girl tried to get in but the doors were bolted. Went out and followed her past the Zwemmer Gallery and through the streets towards St Giles' only to lose her by the Cambridge Theatre, cursing the upbringing which after all these years has left me unable to address a stranger. Much disturbed by the incident, for this girl, with her high forehead, her pointed nose, her full lips and fine eyes, her dark hair and her unhappy sullen expression, personified both beauty and intelligence in distress. She was bare-legged, and wore sandals, a green corduroy suit and a linen coat.

Apropos of that wartime Julie Christie, my empathy with Connolly was perfect. Me too! Girls glimpsed, followed with no malign intent, but only mute longing, though not, alas, in the streets between the Zwemmer Gallery and the Cambridge Theatre. Other evocations of place and atmosphere were more exotic, and all the better for it. There were, for example, The Beaches Of The West.

Houlgate, Royan, Saint-Jean-de-Luz. A red digue, colour of porphry. In the shops are hanging buckets, toy yachts, shrimping nets and string bags enclosing rubber balls with a dull bloom, of the same porphry colour. Children in the shops are choosing sandals and gym-shoes, girls are walking arm-in-arm along the promenade: the west wind from the sea spatters the jetty stones with rain; old bills of casino galas with their faded 'Attractions' roll flapping among the tamarisks. Prowling from the Marquise de Sévigné tea room to the Pontinière bar, dark and smelling of gin, we lie in wait for one more glimpse of the sea-side girls in their impregnable adolescence – before the Atlantic sun fades angrily over enormous sands, coloured like the under-belly of soles.

There was enough here of the familiar to give me a general purchase on the scene, Donaghadee for toy yachts and rubber beach balls, Portstewart for enormous sands and the angry Atlantic sun, Newcastle for old bills of departed pierrots, and impregnable, adolescent, seaside girls *passim*. But the glamour of it all! Digues! Tamarisks! The Beaches Of The West!

Then there were Houses In The Country:

The morning awakening of a house, voices of women in a courtyard, the chickens, ducks, geese and dogs being let out; the smell of breakfast, the gardener bringing in tomatoes and lettuces; Sunday papers, taps running; and the drone of fighter squadrons overhead. Lunch out of doors. The afternoon nap, so rich in memory disturbances: the bath in fading twilight with water pipes rumbling and shrieks of children going to bed, while the cold elmy sunshine westers over liquid fields. The sharp bedtime sortie into the night air. It is only in the country that we can get to know a person or a book.

My mother and I were sometimes invited into the country to stay with the families of farmers who had known my mother before the Second World War and who sympathised with us in our sad circumstances. But it was a strain to try to equate this sort of thing with Connolly. There was no courtyard, no gardener, no Sunday papers, no *al fresco*, no siesta, no bath (no taps), no sorties, no persons worth getting to know, no books except the Good Book. For these were farmhouses rather than Houses In The Country and I have a feeling that the sunshine was not elmy nor were the fields liquid. I tried to romanticise if nothing else the simplicity of those early days, the farmer and the farmer's wife and the farmer's wife's mother and ourselves at bedtime, reading a chapter of Scripture verse by verse, turn and turn about while the bright paraffin lamps hummed against the whitewashed walls of the kitchen. Then, after a short word of prayer from the farmer, upstairs to an early bed in bedrooms where the massive beds and wardrobes and tallboys seemed to take up all the space: a Wooden Age (in Connolly's phrase), ewers of water on drawers of wood, in mine.

And October On The Mediterranean. What about that!

Blue skies rinsed by the mistral, red and golden vine branches, wind fretted waves chopping round the empty yachts; plane trees peeling; palms rearing up their dingy underclothes.

Ah, that would be the life! When I was nineteen I had these and many other palinurisms by heart, mantras against the longueurs of the morning meeting. While the brethren prayed their two-at-a-time, competitive prayers, I prayed the Connolly prayer. 'Streets of Paris, pray for me; beaches in the sun, pray for me, ghosts of the lemurs intercede for me; plane-tree and laurel-rose shade me; summer rain on quays of Toulon, wash me away.' Some day, I thought, some day I too will be 'peeling off the kilometres to the tune of "Blue Skies", sizzling down the long black liquid stretches of Nationale Sept, the plane trees going sha-sha-sha through the open window, the windscreen yellowing with crushed midges, she with the Michelin beside me, a handkerchief binding her hair ...' Some day ... Meanwhile, how I envied the young Connolly. And, innocent that I was, young Belfast/Plymouth brother, backslidden perhaps, but none unworldlier, how I admired the older Connolly for the realism which allowed him in middle age to remember that the dream girl on the dream journey to the sun had a bit of a spare tyre.

The Unquiet Grave suggested an economical formula for book-making, exciting me as in the days of the titles from Shakespeare. The recipe would seem to be quite simple: transcriptions from books of phrases and paragraphs which pleased, the odd *pensée* of my own, plangent descriptions of the weather, brief encounters, lost horizons.

Grey, still day at the end of March, I drive down the eastern side of Strangford Lough. The sea is shot lead under a drumskin sky. At Portaferry the catatonic gulls brood on their sins.

THE WISDOM OF W. H. AUDEN
Poetry changes nothing.

THE WISDOM OF L. WITTGENSTEIN
Philosophy ... leaves everything as it is ... Philosophy simply puts everything before us, and neither explains or deduces anything – Since everything lies open to view there is nothing to explain.

17th September, Galway: The sea nearly as occidental as cowboys, the full horizon lipping.

17th November: My hypochondria approaches valetudinarianism. This morning I awoke with an unusual sense of well-being, I immediately looked up 'euphoria' in my symptom book.

23rd December: Bitter, cold evening. In DuBarry's, a louche bar down by the docks, the whores, their rough Belfast accents poshed up, softly sing 'I saw Mummy kissing Santa Claus underneath the mistletoe last night'.

The suffering of Christ: the cross on the scree, the double cross in the garden, the double six on the centurion's coat.

THE WISDOM OF PALINURUS

The first signs of a mutual attraction will induce even the inconsolable to live in the present ... Life is a maze in which we take the wrong turning before we have learned to walk ... Fallen leaves lying on the grass in the November sun bring more happiness than daffodils ... Autumn is the mind's true spring.

Autumn in Edinburgh: Running up steep cobbled streets as yellow as arrowroot biscuits in the pale, misty, maturing sun. Down into the darkness of Waverley to buy the *New Statesman* and the *Listener*. Reading book reviews by V. S. Pritchett and John Raymond and Edwin Muir and T. C. Worsley and Maurice Richardson beside the first September fire in the still empty bar of the Adelphi Hotel in Cockburn Street. Then an Arabian Friday night in Milne's with John Tonge and Hugo Moore and Sidney and Hazel and Ian and Agnes and Christopher and Valda and John Reid and John Reid's girlfriend. *Bona fide* travelling in the Scotia Hotel from ten until two. Then the bilges begin to empty.

THE NONSENSE OF GRAHAM GREENE

I have been reading *The Lawless Roads*, Greene's travel book about godless Mexico. In the prologue he revisits Berkhamstead. 'Up the hillside the beech trees were in flamboyant decay: little boxes for litter put up by the National Trust had a dainty and doily effect: and in the inn the radio played continuously. You could not escape it: with your soup a dramatized account of the battle of Mons, and with the joint a Methodist church service. Four one armed men dined together, arranging their seats so that their arms shouldn't clash.' 'Ah, seedy old Greeneland', enthuse the

131

critics. 'Four one-armed men! Where else would they dine to-gether? And does no detail escape that beady eye? Arranging their seats so that their arms shouldn't clash!' But 'clash', which in this context seems to mean only that two forks might knock together, is a silly word. And if the amputations are symmetrical a 'clash' is impossible; if they are asymmetrical it is inevitable.

THE WISDOM OF EDMUND GOSSE

Evangelical religion, or any religion in a violent form ... divides heart from heart. It sets up a vain, chimerical ideal, in the barren pursuit of which all the tender, indulgent affections, all the genial play of life, all the exquisite pleasures and soft resignations of the body, all that enlarges and calms the soul, are exchanged for what is harsh and void and negative. It encourages a stern and ignorant spirit of condemnation; it throws altogether out of gear the healthy movement of the conscience ... it invents sins which are no sins at all, but which darken the heaven of innocent joy with futile clouds of remorse.

When Gosse recalls the vain, chimerical ideal of the brethren together with their consequent stern and ignorant condemnation of all that is soul-enlarging he is surely remembering their attitude towards literature and the arts. When, aged fourteen, he attended his first evangelical conference in London, 'the terrible vastness of the crowd, with rings on rings of dim white faces fading in the fog', he was appalled to hear 'an elderly man, fat and greasy, with a voice like a bassoon and an imperturbable assurance', castigate the Laodiceanism of the contemporary Church, which had failed to denounce the current Shakespearean tercentenary, 'the blasphemous celebration of the birth of Shakespeare, a lost soul now suffering for his sins in hell'. Gosse recalls the innocent comfort he took in his father's mitigation of that judgement, however 'meagre to gay and worldly spirits' the concession might seem. 'Brother So-and-so,' remarked Gosse the elder, 'was not in my judgement justified in saying what he did. The unconvenanted mercies of God are not revealed to us. Before so rashly speaking of Shakespeare as a lost soul in hell, he should have remembered how little we know of the poet's history. The light of salvation was widely disseminated in the land during the reign of Queen Elizabeth, and we cannot know that Shakespeare did not accept the atonement of Christ in simple faith before he came to die.'

Was Shakespeare saved? By the time I was inscribing 'The Wisdom of Edmund Gosse' in my copycat *Unquiet Grave* the question was, as they say, academic, but there was a time when

I would have thought it important, a time when, like Gosse, although 'I was not consciously in revolt against the strict faith in which I was brought up … I could not fail to be aware of the fact that literature tempted me to stray up innumerable paths which meandered in directions at right angles to that direct strait way which leadeth to salvation.' During that time, which was short, I tried to marry strict faith and literary merit through the advocacy of writers whom even the brethren would find hard to fault theologically.

There was of course Bunyan, for whom I affected for a while an exaggerated enthusiasm. His account of his conversion was impeccable. 'Then Christian gave three leaps for joy, and went on singing':

> Thus far did I come loaden with my sin,
> Nor could aught ease the grief that I was in,
> Till I came hither. What a place is this!
> Must here be the beginning of my bliss?
> Must here the burden fall from off my back?
> Must here the strings that bound it to me crack?
> Blessed Cross! Blessed Sepulchre! Blessed rather be
> The man that there was put to shame for me.

And the good Dr Johnson:

> DR ADAMS: What do you mean by 'damned'? JOHNSON: (passionately and loudly) Sent to hell, Sir, and punished eternally.

These were the brethren's sentiments exactly. But above all there was George Herbert, for whom my enthusiasm was genuine and who was surely quotable even in the morning meeting.

> Love bade me welcome; but my soul drew back,
>   Guilty of dust and sin.
> But quick-ey'd Love, observing me grow slack
>   From my first entrance in,
> Drew nearer to me, sweetly questioning
>   If I lacked any thing.

Or, if the sexual allusion should seem overexplicit, (to the puritan all things are impure):

> Only a sweet and virtuous soul
> Like season'd timber, never gives;
> But though the whole world turn to coal,
>   Then chiefly lives.

Sir Walter Ralegh might serve a turn, but only in parts.

> Give me my scallop-shell of quiet,
> My staff of faith to walk upon,
> My scrip of joy, immortal diet,
> My bottle of salvation,
> My gown of glory, hope's true gage,
> And thus I'll take my pilgrimage.

A gown of glory and a staff of faith ('Thy rod and Thy staff') would be perfectly acceptable, but a bottle of salvation was not exactly a brethren concept, salvation being from, rather than of, the bottle.

Modern writers were certainly more difficult. There was always T. S. Eliot. It might go down well to refer to our gospel hall as a place where prayer has been valid – all those conversions in the main hall subsequent to prayer meetings in the back room. And 'The Hippopotamus', suitably bowdlerised, might be good for a scold about these 'last Laodicean days' when 'there are too many who believe that the church can feed and sleep at once. We must work, brethren, for the night is coming.' From *The Rock*, 'Decent godless people' with an emphasis on the 'godless', 'their only monument a thousand lost golf balls' might be the basis of an effective smack at nominal Christendom, washing the car on Sunday morning, out on the links in the afternoon. Vachell Lindsay's 'General William Booth Enters into Heaven', quoted selectively, would probably raise a sentimental tear.

> And when Booth halted by the curb for prayer
> He saw his Master through the flag-filled air.

135

Christ came gently with a robe and crown
For Booth the soldier, while the crowd knelt down.
He saw King Jesus. They were face to face
And he fell a-weeping in that holy place.
Are you washed in the blood of the lamb?

Then there was C. S. Lewis whose stylish casuistry sustained me for a while when my faith began to falter. Pride is certainly a comic emotion and at that time I was proud of Lewis, much as a Roman Catholic might be proud of having such great men as Graham Greene and Evelyn Waugh on his side. Now, nearly forty years later, I still feel something of this when I hear Lewis praised by famous non-believers. For example, Kingsley Amis, remembering the absurd Kenneth Tynan, writes:

> Ken's early choice of heroes shows an unerring capacity to single out shams or worse. Wilhelm Reich, Sid Field, Charlie Chaplin, Adlai Stevenson, Orson Welles, Bertold Brecht – dare I add Hemingway? – with C. S. Lewis, his Oxford tutor, a lonely and startling exception.

Lewis preferred by Amis to Hemingway and Brecht! I glow at the memory of this distinguished Ulster Christian who was not ashamed to proclaim his belief in salvation and damnation and heaven and hell and miracles and the resurrection and second coming of Jesus Christ in glory – one of us or, well, almost one of us.

However, all too soon I knew that the books that interested me could not be sold to the brethren as spiritually uplifting. 'Hale knew they meant to murder him before he had been in Brighton three hours.' Could I explain to the brethren that although *Brighton Rock* might at first reading seem somewhat a strange topic to draw lessons of religion from, nevertheless it contained matter which every young Christian should ponder; that Pinkie as a baptised Roman Catholic (a what?) was nearer to both salvation and damnation than the good-hearted prostitute (the what?) Ida Arnold who knew the difference between right and wrong but nothing of the difference between good and evil? Not really.

It was with some justice, then, that my mother suspected that the books I was reading were doing me no good at all. She resented them as a disruptive and worldly intrusion into a household which had never had any use for such things. Wordsworth and Tennyson and Milton and Shakespeare were doubtless necessary for 'my course'; in addition, they said wise and true things like 'More things are wrought by prayer than this world dreams of' and 'The Devil can cite Scripture for his purpose' and 'There are more things in heaven and earth ... than are dreamt of in your philosophy' and 'How sharper than a serpent's tooth it is to have a thankless child'. But James Joyce? Was he on the course? Was he necesary?

Just the other day she had opened that green book, what do you call it, Ulysses, just opened it at random, and what was the first thing she read? 'Greater love than this, he said, no man hath that a man lay down his wife for a friend.' That was filthy. Worse, it was blasphemous, since it was making a mockery of the very words of our Lord Jesus Christ Himself. Bobbie Wright, once again on furlough from his missionary labours in Japan, shook his head sadly when he saw my copies of Ulysses and Finnegans Wake in their bright new dust wrappers. 'That man had a very dirty mind.' I could hardly protest, 'I know not the man,' but I had nothing to say in defence of my hero. I had not then read what only the very knowledgeable had read, the Dublin letters to Nora which, according to Lady Snow, so shocked her friend Rosemary Mizener the wife of the biographer when she first saw them in the library at Cornell. 'As we left the vaults of the library to return across a snow-covered campus, Rosemary was looking shaken. "I don't think I shall ever forget those letters," she said.' Had I been so privileged I could at least have answered Bobbie with some confidence: 'He certainly had. You don't know the half of it.'

Somewhat in the spirit of Stephen introducing Mrs Daedalus to Ibsen I suggested that my mother might like to read some of these books: Forrest Reid's *Apostate*, Joyce's *Stephen Hero* and, of course, *Father and Son*. This was foolish. When she came to the passage in *Stephen Hero* where Mrs Daedalus berates Stephen for his apostasy, I suspect that she must, as I had intended her to do, have strongly identified her own emotions with the grief and indignation of Mrs Daedalus:

> I little thought that it would come to this – that a child of mine would lose the faith ... I suspected that something was wrong but I never thought ... I do not know what led you astray unless it was those books you read ... You were religiously brought up in a Catholic home ... Think of your own life when you believed ... Weren't you better and happier then ... I know what is wrong with you – you suffer from the pride of the intellect. You think you can defy God because you have misused the talents he has given you ... I suppose you fell in with some of those students ... I never thought I would see the day when a child of mine would lose the faith. God knows I didn't. I did my best for you to keep you in the right way ... I knew no good would come of your going to that place ... You are ruining yourself body and soul. Now your faith is gone.

In all essentials I believe that these were my mother's unspoken thoughts. Suspicions ... those books ... happier then ... pride ... those students ... that place ... never thought I'd see the day. With the substitution of 'Christian home' for 'Catholic home' and some addenda about the bereaved, crippled state in which she had perforce to do her best with no father to guide me, it could have been my mother's speech, and would have been, had my loss of faith ever been as candidly admitted by me or queried by her. However, she suppressed these thoughts and her main reaction was one of indignation that I seemed to be comparing her with an ignorant, superstitious, Roman Catholic woman. 'You think that you are Stephen and I am his mother.' Stephen, it may be remembered, had accused his mother of believing that Jesus was the only man with pure auburn hair, the only man who was exactly six feet tall, neither more nor less. My mother seized on this. 'We don't believe things like that.'

'But you do believe that God literally took a rib out of Adam's body and made a woman out of it?'

'Of course I do.'

'And you do believe that men ever after have had one rib fewer than women?'

'Well, isn't that true? Isn't that the proof of it?'

'Oh, Mother! Don't be absurd!'

Like Mrs Daedalus in the matter of the six-foot, auburn-haired Jesus, she seemed about to 'defend the tradition in a half-hearted way – That is what they say.' Then she shrugged, as if realising that she was vulnerable on the empirical question and that after all it sounded none too plausible.

Her reaction to *Father and Son* was similar. It was of course sad that Edmund had been brought up in that lonely, restricted style (without a mother) but that was all in another century and how different was the home life of our dear boy. There could be no doubt that his father was a sincere, Christian gentleman who meant well, but his views were extreme. In evidence, she referred to Philip Gosse's attitude to Christmas. 'The very word is Popish, Christ's Mass!' She turned up the description of Christmas Day 1857 when, Mr Gosse having forbidden any seasonal change of menu, the servants made an illicit plum pudding and fed a surreptitious slice to young Edmund.

Shortly I began to feel that pain inside which in my frail state was inevitable, and my conscience smote me violently. At length I could bear my spiritual anguish no longer, and bursting into the study I called out: 'Oh! Papa, Papa, I have eaten of the flesh offered to idols!' ... Then my Father said 'Where is the accursed thing?' I explained that as much as was left of it was still on the kitchen table. He took me by the hand, and ran with me into the midst of the startled servants, seized what remained of the pudding, and with the plate in one hand and me still tight in the other, ran till he reached the dust heap, when he flung the idolatrous confectionery on the middle of the ashes and then raked it deep down into the mass.

To my mother this clinched the matter. *Father and Son* was an account of a world quite remote from my experience. 'We always had Christmas.'

The passage which with its heavy mental underlining should have stuck out telepathically was neither pointed out by me nor referred to by my mother, but lay between us like a guilty secret.

Let me speak plainly. After my long experience, after my patience and forbearance, I have surely the right to protest against the untruth (would that I could apply to it any other word!) that evangelical religion, or any religion in a violent form, is a wholesome or a valuable or desirable adjunct to human life. It divides heart from heart. It sets up a vain, chimerical ideal, in the barren pursuit of which all the tender, indulgent affections, all the genial play of life, all the exquisite pleasures and soft resignations of the body, all that enlarges and calms the soul, are exchanged for what is harsh and void and negative. It encourages a stern and ignorant spirit of condemnation; it throws altogether out of gear the healthy movement of the conscience; it invents virtues which are sterile and cruel; it invents sins which are no sins at all, but which darken the heaven of innocent joy with futile clouds of remorse.

There is something horrible, if we will bring ourselves to face it, in the fanaticism that can do nothing with this pathetic and fugitive existence of ours but treat it as if it were the uncomfortable ante-chamber to a palace which no one has explored and of the plan of which we know absolutely nothing. My father, it is true, believed that he was intimately acquainted with the form and furniture of this habitation, and he wished me to think of nothing else but of the advantages of an eternal residence in it.

Re-reading these paragraphs many years later I will admit to finding the tone sometimes extravagant – 'this pathetic and fugitive existence of ours' – the 'heaven of innocent joy' darkened. But when I was nineteen years old, Gosse, *c'était moi*. How I longed to protest my agnosticism about the form and furniture of the hereafter, to name my mother, my relatives, Mr Gibson Stevenson, Mr Moses Bartholomew and all as fanatics, to castigate evangelical religion as unwholesome (though my mother would surely have told me that she did not have a religion, *she* had Christ) above all, to sigh world-wearily: Let me speak plainly. After my long experience, after my patience and forbearance … But I held my peace.

For years after I had become to the best of my belief a convinced atheist, with not the slightest residual doubt, still less any fear that there might be at least some grain of truth in the brethren's crazy *Weltanschauung*, I continued to bow in the House of Rimmon, attending conferences and meetings (my mother leaning on my arm), actually praying in prayer meetings and preaching the gospel both in the open air and in the gospel halls.

Why? I would have said at the time, and I still think the answer is fairly near the truth, that I was extremely conscious of my mother's plight. She never missed an opportunity to make me aware of it, but to be fair, her condition did surely make her a legitimate object of concern, none better placed to feel sorry for her, none more obliged to pity her than myself.

I was the only child, worse, the only son of a widowed mother who had lost one leg and had little use of the other and whose whole ambition, she would have said, was only to see me go on in the ways of the Lord, following in the footsteps of my sainted, tragically dead father. She would tell me, not only once, and always as if she was doing me a great, unselfish favour, that like Hannah with the infant Samuel, she had lent me to the Lord (1 Samuel 1:28). When the brethren sang

Can a mother's tender care
Cease towards the child she bare?
Yes, she may forgetful be,
Yet will I remember Thee,

my mother kept her silence thereby indicating, I suppose, that such a response on her part would be absurd since for her the question could be only rhetorical. The silliest things made her grieve. For example, she wept when, aged fifteen, I gave up physics and chemistry in favour of French and Spanish, thus cutting off my path to a medical degree and a mission in the Copperbelt. How could I do such a thing to myself (and to her)? No triumphal furlough addresses, enthralling the Easter crowds at Glengall Street, could now be anticipated – no heart-rending stories of how M'Gombo had been delivered, appendix and soul, from the machinations of the witch doctor.

In this matter I compared most unfavourably with a young acquaintance in the Knightsbridge assembly, Fred Stanley Arnott Stevenson, son of Gibson Stevenson, the man from the Pru who raised the hymns and prayed somewhat aggressively. Fred was already well on his way to medical school, and if his ambitions were not directed towards the Copperbelt it was only because he had conceived a rather special, indeed a unique exercise towards a neglected sector, the very rich. He had already confided to me and to his special mentor, Moses Bartholomew's son, Aaron, his hope that in the pursuit of this end he would be able to specialise in psychological medicine, eventually becoming a psychoanalyst. That a young fundamentalist Christian (*circa* 1947) should have entertained any ambitions in that direction may seem odd, but his motives were of the very purest.

There were some exceedingly well-off people, he explained to me, who would actually go to a psychoanalyst complaining of feelings of incapacitating guilt, sometimes accompanied by a fear of hell and damnation. The analyst would explain to his clients that these feelings of guilt were irrational and would disappear only when in dialogue with a skilful therapist their origins came to be properly understood. What an opportunity, thought Fred, to speak a word in season to some who might otherwise never hear the gospel, a parish of rich women whose eternal prospects were as uncertain as those of the average camel attempting to negotiate the eye of a needle. Fred would tell the rich patients who came to his consulting rooms the truth, that, far from being irrational, their feelings of guilt were well founded, being the proper response to their desperate situation. They were indeed guilty sinners, estranged from a righteous God and on their way to hell, and the only remedy was recognition of their guilt, repentance from their sins and faith in the atoning work of Jesus Christ. He did not tell me if he thought a hundred guineas would be an appropriate fee for such uniquely excellent advice.* Quite unfitted to follow Fred, how then could I deny my mother a merely cosmetic submission to the ways of the brethren, which meant so much to her, when she had already suffered so much?

I considered my own situation, not I fear without some adolescent self-pity and a good deal of *mauvaise foi* in the excuses I made to myself for continuing therein. It seemed to me about as bad as it could be. If only there had been a brother or a sister with whom to spread the burden then surely, I told myself, I would have gone my own way. Or if I had been my mother's daughter, then without what I convinced myself was an additional Oedipean complexity, I would have outfaced her, woman to woman, calling her emotional bluff. More plausibly, if it had been my father rather than my mother who had survived to be my tormentor with his other-worldly, professedly disinterested ambitions for me, surely I would have been able to cope; to tell him straight out that while he might be marching to Zion, the beautiful city of God, most assuredly I was not, even though such defiance would certainly have turned his moisture into the

* [If at that time I had been asked that question I would have replied that I intended to earn my living as a general practitioner in the mornings, devoting my afternoons to this special ministry the Lord had laid on my heart, 'for His name's sake ... taking nothing of the Gentiles' (3 John 7) but expounding the gospel 'without money and without price' (Isaiah 55:1) – *F.S.A.S.*]

drought of summer, Selah. Gosse, escaped to London, although consumed with despair at his own feebleness and want of will (my feelings exactly), together with pity for his father's obvious distress, managed to cope with Philip Gosse's 'postal inquisition'. 'When your sainted Mother died, she not only tenderly committed you to God, but left you also as a solemn charge to me, to bring you up in the nurture and admonition of the Lord. That responsibility I have kept constantly before me.... Before your childhood was past, there seemed God's manifest blessing on our care; for you seemed truly converted to Him; you confessed in solemn baptism that you had died and been raised with Christ; and you were received with joy into the bosom of the Church of God, as one alive from the dead' and so on and so on and so on.

Substitute a sainted father for a sainted mother and I could well imagine my mother's tearful litany, subsequent on any overt apostasy of mine, at once more incoherent than Gosse's and because of that so much harder to deal with: tender commitment, solemn charge, responsibility, conversion, baptism, reception into the bosom of the Church of God. 'How can I go up to my Father (to say nothing of *your father*) in heaven and the lad be not with me?' Only a very heartless lad would have been impervious to such a plea.

I also recognised that the greatest handicap of all was my mother's physical condition. From very early days, while still at preparatory school, still a believer, trusting Jesus most of the time (doubting days always excepted), I was resentful of and deeply ashamed of my mother's broken frame – and full of guilt that I should feel such resentment and shame against and for a state for which she was blameless. Her frequent references to her condition filled me with unease. When she left hospital and went to live on the Stranmillis Road, the rector of St Bartholomew's Church of Ireland church visited her, wondering if she might be a new parishioner. My mother told him her sad story. She then

145

explained that as a simple, born-again Christian, saved when she was a little girl aged only ten, who had learned the biblical truth about believers' baptism and assembly fellowship according to New Testament principles, she had no need for the rituals of the so-called churches. Did Dr Lindsay, she wondered, know and love the Lord Jesus Christ as his own and personal saviour? Nettled, the rector took his leave, asking her if she expected in heaven to be reunited with her errant limb as well as with my father. The story was told over and over again, as the saints exclaimed at the shocking behaviour of a minister of Christ (so-called), but I fear I was less appalled by the rector's rudeness than by my mother's unashamed reference in mixed company to her missing leg. Why did she have to be so explicit? Why did she have to talk about it at all? When she confided in me, as she frequently did, that she had a bad pain in her stump today, I was disgusted, and dismayed that I should be disgusted. Stump! What a word! The only stumps I wanted to know about had bails on them. Thus to my lasting shame were my teeth set on edge, like the teeth of those children in the Book of Jeremiah whose fathers had eaten a sour grape.

On a hot July day just after the end of the Second World War she came to school for the Father's Day cricket match to watch me play. Cars and petrol were still in short supply but all the parents at Cabin Hill seemed to have been able to lay their hands on at least a taxi. My mother would have said she could not afford one, and so taking two trams she toiled across Belfast, finally limping up the half-mile of the school drive with her heavy stick and her artificial leg, shod in ugly black boots. She watched the game uncomprehending, and at teatime was fussed over by a non-playing prefect, more gracious than I. (Easy for him, I thought, she's not his mother.) When my friend Spender (whose father Captain Spender, on leave from a good war in Whitehall had just made 33 not out) later remarked, ingenuously or disingenuously, that he had seen me with my granny, I did not dispute the description. The match over, I had to give her my arm and walk her back to the main road while private cars and taxis, Austin Twelves and Standard Tens, Humbers and Rileys, an Alvis, an Armstrong-Siddeley rolled down the hill past us. As she limped off and hoisted herself onto the tram I recognised that it would be wicked in anyone, and beyond belief in me, a sinner saved by grace, to wish that she had stayed at home. But I did, fervently. For a father dropping catches and coming in at the ninth wicket, for two parents with four legs evenly distributed in a Sunbeam Talbot I would have dealt with Mephistopheles.

So, four years later, how was I to say to her that the beliefs of the brethren were unmitigated nonsense? That at death the dome of many-coloured glass is trampled to fragments, the million-petalled flower of being here disintegrates, the insubstantial pageant fades, leaving not a rack behind. No heaven, no hell, no salvation, no damnation, no lake burning with fire and brimstone, no glad reunion with my father, no great advantage to be gained from keeping out of picture houses. When, further years on, I did eventually stammer some of these things in a half-hearted way, her reaction was what I had suspected all along that it would be: not alarm at my eternal damnation but dismay at what relatives and fellow saints in the assembly would say and think. Her exact words were what I felt I had always known they would be: 'How can you do this thing to me when I have already suffered so much?' What she dreaded was the false pity, the *Schadenfreude* of the closed community ('Of course she should never have sent him to that school'), the clammy prayers of visiting elders for the backslider.

Therefore I procrastinated. Owl-solemn, under the street lights on lonely city walks, I could identify strongly with Stephen Daedalus's young friend Cranly:

> They paced along three sides of the Green in silence while the couples began to leave the chains and return to their modest resting places and after a while Cranly began to explain to

147

Stephen how he too had felt a desire for life – a life of freedom and happiness – when he had been younger and how at that time he too had been about to leave the Church in search of happiness but that many considerations had constrained him.

Constrained then, like Cranly, by many considerations, I had been drawn more and more into practices which both embarrassed and shamed me. After the march round the houses to advertise the Sunday evening gospel meeting, the brethren would retire, to have a prayer meeting, to the small room at the back of the gospel hall where I had so recently been dried off. Here, in almost identical words, those simple men would pray, turn and turn about, for the success of the gospel meeting about to begin. Almighty God, our Heavenly Father, they would invariably begin. Then they would boldly approach the throne of grace (Hebrews 4:16) that they might obtain mercy and find grace to help in time of need. The speaker, Thy servant, our brother, would be brought before the Lord, that his arms might be strengthened and the fear of man (Proverbs 29:25) removed, as he sought faithfully to bear witness yet again to the saving power of the finished work at Calvary. As the hymn writer had put it so beautifully, it is finished yes indeed, finished every jot, sinner this is all you need, tell me is it not? Might our brother be granted the power of the Spirit to speak a word in season which would fall into good ground bringing forth fruit, thirtyfold, sixtyfold, even a hundredfold to the glory of God (Matthew 13:8). As the hymn writer had written, Mercy drops round us were falling but what we pleaded for was showers of blessing. Almighty God was reminded that it was not His will that any should perish but that all should come to repentance (2 Peter 3:9), that His hand was not shortened that it could not save nor was His ear heavy that it could not hear (Isaiah 59:1). Optimistic mention would be made of those friends who might come in off the street, perhaps to hear the gospel for the first time, and, more realistically, of named individuals, the children of believers,

148

who would certainly be present, that young Malcolm Bleaney for example, that child of many prayers, might this very evening close with God's offer of salvation, accepting that Christ had died in his guilty room and stead (never 'instead of him' but always 'in his room and stead'). Finally, support would be invoked for the gospel wherever it was preached this evening, to earth's remotest bounds, that wherever Christ was lifted up to the gaze of the perishing, men would be drawn to Him (John 12:32). All this would be asked in the Name of, and for the sake of Thy Son, our Saviour, the Lord Jesus Christ.

There were not many of us, and I would keep a furtive eye on my watch hoping that the half-hour of prayer would be filled and to spare by senior suppliants. All too often, however, by ten minutes to seven all the saints in the little room except me would have prayed. There would be a long silence when sighs short and frequent were exhaled, interspersed with the odd pious groan, indicative of some private wrestling. Then one of the elders would get to his feet signalling that we might all rise, dusting off the knees of our trousers. Reproachful looks, so it seemed to me, were directed at the non-participant.

And so, not too many Sunday evenings after I was baptised, I was dismayed to hear myself boldly approaching the throne of grace to find help in time of need for Thy servant our brother that he might be granted a word in season and enabled to lift up Christ to the gaze of the perishing, since it was not God's will that any should perish but that all should come to repentance – that the gospel to earth's remotest bounds might prosper and wherever Christ was lifted to the gaze of the perishing, men might be drawn to Him – all these requests being understood to have been made in the Name of, and for the sake of Thy Son, our Saviour the Lord Jesus Christ. This performance was amen-ed much more enthusiastically than any of the regular contributions, both during the prayer and after, when all the brethren loudly said 'Amen!', two of them twice. They were not, of course, moved to

149

such a fulsome endorsement by my eloquence, but were in their artless way saying, 'Well done!' I curled my toes until I thought they would go into cramp.

As the years went by, further participations were exacted. I avoided the commitment to take a Sunday school class on the grounds that my attendances while I was at boarding school would be too irregular to permit such an undertaking. But on the Sundays when I was in attendance I went to the so-called Bible Class, which was devoted to scriptural exposition for saved young people, and which was held in a corner of the hall at the same time as the Sunday school. So if, as often happened, some brother or sister who was a regular Sunday school teacher was absent, I would be asked to supply the need and could hardly refuse. On these occasions much of the time could be spent in hearing the children's verses. They would be required to learn a chapter by heart, say John chapter 3, or Romans chapter 5, a verse at a time. So if I was in luck they might have progressed as far as John 3 and 36, which involved a lot of timeconsuming recitation, all the way from 'There was a man of the Pharisees, named Nicodemus' to 'he that believeth not the Son shall not see the life; but the wrath of God abideth on him'. The children of the brethren would be well drilled and even if the lesser breeds were totally unprepared, I was ready to prompt them at every other word through the thirty-six verses, so putting in half an hour. Those who were waiting to recite or who had already performed became bored and fought with one another. But since such confusion was general all over the hall it was not something for which I felt I need hold myself responsible. If they had just started their chapter, I filled the time by telling them Bible stories, David and Goliath, Moses in Egypt, Joseph in Egypt, Jacob and Esau, Joshua and Jericho, Daniel in the den of lions. Aged fifteen, I found the duty of telling ten-year-olds that they needed to be born again quite beyond me, so at no time did I urge God's plan of salvation on those whom the elderly superintendent quaintly referred to as the 'scholars'.

On Wednesday evenings during the summer months, the younger brethren would assemble at the gospel hall for a short prayer meeting preparatory to an excursion with the gospel message into darkest Edenderry or Lambeg or Dundonald or Newtownbreda or Holywood or Mossley. This exercise was known as the Village Work and seems to have been a tradition in most of the working-class assemblies in Belfast, going back to the early years of the century when these places really were villages and not dormitory towns or suburbs in the Belfast conurbation. Great missionary brethren grown famous in Angola or the Belgian Congo would tell at conference time how during the First World War they had on such a foray spoken their first stumbling words in the gospel. (And hadn't they come on!) Clearly it was an environment that might have been made for the tyro, a hunting part of young males, far from the inhibiting presence of elders and women and mothers. So I was frequently egged on to have a go, that is to say, encouraged to witness for my Lord. As, eventually, I did, on a cold, windy evening in August, shouting the gospel message into a terrace of two-up two-down houses, the doors of which were all tightly shut against it. 'Hebrews chapter nine and verse twenty-seven,' I screamed. 'It is appointed unto men once to die, but after death the judgment. Hebrews nine and twenty-two: Without shedding of blood is no remission. The Gospel According to John chapter three and verse seven,' I yelled, 'Marvel not that I say unto thee, Ye must be born again.' All this was heard only by the amen-ing brethren and a small boy with his dog, my Nicodemus, who, far from marvelling, did not so much as blink at the obstetric absurdity. 'Is it nothing to you, all ye that pass by?' I bleated, but there were no passers-by, only rain in the wind, and soon it began to spit. So big Jim Sheridan gave the last short word, briefly advised everyone 'within the sound of my voice' to remember Lot's wife ('Luke seventeen and thirty-two'), shouted a prayer that God would in his rich mercy save some listener, and we went home.

The next assignment on offer was the opening of the gospel meeting. The elder whose month it was, as the brethren said, that is who was currently responsible for providing a Sunday evening speaker, would ask me if I would like to open the meeting for brother So-and-so. For months after such a proposal was first mooted I demurred, but in the end I succumbed. This introduction involved a rubric which, though unwritten, was never departed from. A hymn, a prayer ('Let us bow our heads in prayer'), another hymn, the announcement of forthcoming attractions, Bible Reading on Tuesday at eight, prayer meeting on Thursday at eight, gospel meeting next Lord's Day at seven when we look forward to welcoming our brother So-and-so from the assembly at Such-and-such, never forgetting to add that all these meetings would be held ('of course') only in the will of the Lord, or if the Lord tarry (nothing so offhand as 'DV'). Then, we were very glad to have with us this evening our esteemed brother X from Y and it was our prayer that he would experience God's richest blessing as he sought to bring us a message in the gospel, lifting up Christ to the gaze of the perishing.

This exercise did not leave much scope for originality in the apprentice, except perhaps in the hymns he chose to give out. Not always even that, for sometimes the preacher would supply, because they were relevant to his forthcoming message, the hymns he wanted to be announced. More usually he did not, and so he could refer during his sermon to the hymns with which our young brother had started the meeting with their striking relevance to the message the Lord had given him. Here was evidence that the Holy Spirit had had a hand in the affair since, in the matching of hymns to text and sermon, there had been no collusion between His servants on the platform. On a rare occasion the evangelist might even announce that, although he had come to the meeting prepared to speak on something quite different, he had felt most strongly during the singing of our young brother's opening hymn with those beautiful words

– 'The Spirit and the Bride say come, and drink of the water of life!' – that the Holy Spirit was laying it on his heart to expound a passage of Scripture which had not even been in his mind at all when he entered the gospel hall. So, if we would open our bibles at the prophecy of Isaiah, chapter 55, beginning to read at the first verse, 'Ho, every one that thirsteth, come ye to the waters, and he that hath no money; come ye, buy, and eat; yea, come, buy wine and milk without money and without price.' A proud moment for the young brother, and the brethren thought well of a man able and willing to speak off the cuff at the bidding of the Spirit.

Next, I would be asked if, as well as opening the meeting, I would like, myself, to say a few words in the gospel, perhaps to give my testimony. Visiting speakers, unless very distinguished, were always tolerant of, indeed enthusiastic towards a young Christian willing to share the platform and bear witness for the first time. So, in the fullness of time, sixteen years old, embarrassed (what the brethren called the fear of man) I felt compelled to relate the story of my conversion.

Well then, what a great privilege it had been to have been brought up in a Christian home, the only child of Godly parents who had prayed for me even before I was born, a child of many prayers indeed, sung to sleep with the songs of Zion. Not of course that such a privileged upbringing could ever of itself fit its recipient for heaven. On the contrary, the privilege placed on him a dreadful, indeed an awesome, responsibility. For as we read in the Gospel According to Luke, chapter 12 and verse 48, unto whomsoever much is given, of him shall much be required. Ah no, my sinner friends might rest assured, Godly upbringing notwithstanding, I too had been on the downward path to a lost eternity, a guilty, hell-deserving sinner who needed to be born again. As the hymn writer had put it:

Ye must be born again
Or never enter Heaven.

'Tis only blood bought ones are there,
The ransomed and forgiven.

I would never forget that winter evening in the Gospel Hall, Railway Street, Strabane, when under the solemn ministry of our dearly beloved brother Mr Willoughby, now gone to be with the Lord he loved and served so well, I became convinced that the Lord's coming was drawing very nigh, that he might come at any time, that he might come perhaps that very night, leaving me behind for the righteous sentence of a just God, eternity in hell and the Lake of Fire, my last chance gone for ever. At the close of the meeting I had been in a state of great distress and Mr Willoughby had knelt with me in prayer and then opened the Scriptures at the Book of the Prophet Isaiah and like Philip with the Ethiopian eunuch all those years ago he had expounded to me chapter 53, reading to me that beautiful verse: 'But he was wounded for our transgressions, he was bruised for our iniquities: the chastisement of our peace was upon him; and with his stripes we are healed'. The verse had been of course long familiar to me, one I had known from my youth up, but for the first time (a downright lie, this) I had realised that it was MY iniquities and MY transgressions that had nailed the blessed Son of God to the tree (My! My! the ubiquitous first-person singular of brethren hymns and preaching). And so I had closed with God's offer of a full and free pardon for all my many sins. As the hymn writer had put it so beautifully:

My sin! Oh the bliss of the glorious thought!
My sin, not in part, but the whole!
Is nailed to His cross and I bear it no more,
It is well! It is well with my soul!

Oh glad and glorious Gospel!
With joy we now proclaim
A full and free salvation
Through faith in Jesus' Name.

154

Ever since, I had experienced the peace which passeth all understanding, the peace of knowing that all my sins were forgiven, and that, if I were to die tonight, I could rest assured that I would go straight to heaven, that to be absent from the body was only to be present with the Lord, Second Corinthians 5 and 8, as my sinner friends in the gospel hall too might come to know this very evening, if only they would acknowledge their guilty, hell-deserving condition, repent and turn in simple faith to the atoning work of Jesus Christ on Calvary.

> Three crosses standing side by side,
> Of broken law a sign.
> Two for their own transgressions died,
> The middle One for mine.

The visiting preacher said 'Amen!' and I sat down feeling rather sick. Small wonder. It is not so much 'privileged upbringing', 'simple faith', 'sinner friends', 'hell-deserving condition', 'songs of Zion', 'the peace which passeth all understanding' or even what the hymn writer had put so beautifully: it is the memory of being sixteen years old and actually saying out loud the words, 'our dearly beloved brother Mr Willoughby, now gone to be with the Lord he loved and served so well' that is still so potent to embarrass.

During the subsequent years, while my nascent doubts blossomed into full-blown incredulity, I was a not infrequent performer, on one occasion opening the meeting in a loft near the Gobelins Métro for our man in Vitry-sur-Seine, Bertie Beattie from the Oldpark. Nobody got saved that evening, perhaps because the audience had been more than ordinarily puzzled by what they heard from me about the big thank-you of a good God towards a poor, miserable fisherman.

I never advanced, though often pressed to, from the role of subsidiary to that of principal. During one such prolegomenon, however, young Malcolm Bleaney, now aged eighteen, was, to my great dismay, led to Christ. At the close of the meeting he insisted that he had got saved and, furthermore, not during the main sermon by the visiting evangelist but as a result of something I had said while warming up –

Two for their own transgressions died,
The middle One for mine.

– which had become something of a nervous tic with me, like Mr Gibson Stevenson's recitation of the verses allegedly written by the lunatic.

The preacher that Sunday evening, a top man, was not perhaps best pleased, although he affected to share what must surely be my great joy in having led my first soul to Christ. He well remembered how he himself had felt, more than thirty years ago now, when at the little gospel hall on the Shimna Road in Newcastle he had had the inestimable privilege of winning his first sinner for his Lord. He adapted, as the brethren were wont to do on such occasions, the words of a famous soul-winner of the past, Samuel Rutherford, author of *The Sands of Time are Sinking*, who had apparently once said:

If one soul from Anworth
Meet me at God's right hand,
My heaven will be two heavens
In Immanuel's land.

So, if one soul from the Shimna Road ... if one soul from the Knightsbridge Gospel Hall, Sunshine Street, meet me at God's right hand ... Winning souls for Christ was of course the chief end, purpose, *raison d'être* of the believer's life, and there would be something of a lacuna in the *curriculum vitae* of the saint who had not been the instrument (under God) of pointing at least one sinner to Jesus. Now, at missionary conference time, I need no longer feel embarrassed or perhaps guilty when the saints sang:

Must I go, and empty-handed,

Must I meet my Saviour so?
Not one soul with which to greet Him,
Must I empty-handed go?

I would no longer be empty-handed for I would be bringing young Malcolm, a feather in my cap, a star in my crown.

'May I introduce Malcolm Bleaney, Lord, a brand plucked from the burning, having been saved under my ministry on the twelfth of February, nineteen-fifty-one?'

'Oh! Well done, thou good and faithful servant. Clearly thou hast not hidden thy talent in a napkin nor hast thou buried it in the sand, hast thou? Enter into the joy of thy Lord. Oh! and be a ruler over five cities.'

Amid all the general euphoria I felt it was not up to me to point out that Malcolm might after all be only a professor, but I thought his mother might have had the decency to do so, introducing the to me welcome possibility that all was not yet lost since Malcolm might not be saved. He was no more than six months younger than I was, and beginning to acquire among the saints a reputation for being difficult, for being a reluctant attender at special gospel meetings who no longer sang the hymns heartily or looked the speaker in the eye or kept his eyes shut while we were praying. Poor Mrs Bleaney was reputedly finding him a bit of a handful, and old Thomas Bleaney with his doubts was not a useful role model. Perhaps Malcolm was pulling my leg. I must have looked shifty, but nobody seemed to notice. Was he winking?

It did not last. Within six months the professor was walking out with an unsaved girl and within a year he was on probation for stealing bicycles. Still, it was a close-run thing, which should, you might think, have given me pause. But years later I was still at it, preaching, if not exactly in season and out of season (2 Timothy 4:2), at least now and then, a dog turned again and again to its vomit and a sow to her wallowing in the mire (2 Peter 2:22).

As peculiar people we were always conscious of the world out there beyond the sequestered confines of our restricted lives, with its alluring fripperies, its seductive temptations, aware of an almost Platonic distinction between the things which were seen and so merely temporal and the things which were unseen and therefore eternal. 'Love not the world, neither the things that are in the world. If any man love the world, the love of the Father is not in him. For all that is in the world, the lust of the flesh ... and the pride of life, is not of the Father, but is of the world' (1 John 2:15–16). As a young believer I was constantly reminded of those twin pitfalls which our adversary Satan, walking about like a roaring lion seeking whom he might devour (1 Peter 5:8), would place in my path, fleshly lust (impurity) and intellectual pride (knowing better than God). However, Edmund Gosse's gradual tergiversation seems to have been a one-sided business, entirely intellectual with no hint of the temptations of the flesh so solemnly alluded to by his older contemporary, Mark Rutherford.

> Impurity was not an excusable weakness in the society in which I lived; it was a sin for which dreadful punishment was reserved. The reason for my virtue may have been a wrong reason, but anyway I was saved, and being saved, much more was saved than health and peace of mind. To this day I do not know where to find a weapon strong enough to subdue the tendency to impurity in young men; and although I cannot tell them what I do not believe, I hanker sometimes for the old prohibitions and penalties.

> Physiological penalties are too remote, and the subtler penalties
> – the degradation, the growth of callousness to finer pleasures,
> the loss of sensitiveness to all that is most nobly attractive in
> woman – are too feeble to withstand temptation when it lies in
> ambush like a garotter, and has the reason stunned in a moment.

Indeed, although Gosse praises his father for the 'uplifted Quixotism' which would not allow him 'to fancy me guilty of any moral misbehaviour, but concentrated his fear entirely on my faith', there is no evidence that the father's solicitude was quixotically misdirected. 'Does the candle of the Lord shine upon your soul? Do you get any spiritual companionship with young men? You passed over last Sunday without a word, yet this day is the most interesting to me in your whole week. Do you find the ministry of the Word pleasant, and above all, profitable? Does it bring your soul into exercise before God? The Coming of Christ draweth nigh. Watch, therefore, and pray always, that you may be accounted worthy to stand before the Son of Man.' These, surely, were the right questions and injunctions to address to a young man who seems to have been in danger of being seduced by nothing sexier than Carlyle and Ruskin – 'those magicians'.

It was the pride of life then, in its most odious exemplification, intellectual arrogance, that was young Gosse's undoing. As the father writes in the last letter recorded by the son:

> When you came to us in the summer, the heavy blow fell full upon
> me; and I discovered how very far you had departed from God.
> It was not that you had yielded to the strong tide of youthful
> blood, and had fallen a victim to fleshly lusts; in that case,
> however sad, your enlightened conscience would have spoken
> loudly and you would have found your way back to the blood
> which cleanseth us from all sin, to humble confession and self-
> abasement, to forgiveness and re-communion with God. It was
> not this; it was worse. It was that horrid, insidious infidelity,
> which had already worked in your mind and heart with terrible

energy. Far worse, I say, because this was sapping the very foundations of faith, on which all true godliness, all real religion, must rest.

Nothing seemed left to which I could appeal. We had, I found, no common ground. The Holy Scriptures had no longer any authority; you had taught yourself to evade their inspiration. Any particular Oracle of God which pressed you, you could easily explain away; even the very character of God you weighed in your balance of fallen reason, and fashioned it accordingly. You were thus sailing down the rapid tide of time towards Eternity, without a single authoritative guide (having cast your chart overboard), except what you might fashion and forge on your own anvil – except what you might *guess*, in fact.

Do not think I am speaking in passion and using unwarrantable strength of words. If the written Word is not absolutely authoritative, what can we know of God? What more than we can infer, that is, guess – as the thoughtful heathen guessed – Plato, Socrates, Cicero – from dim and mute surrounding phenomena?

What do we know of eternity? Of our relations to God? Especially of a *sinner* to God? What of reconciliation? What of the capital question – How can a God of perfect, spotless rectitude deal with me, a corrupt sinner … ?

This dreadful conduct of yours I had intended, after much prayer, to pass over in silence; but your apparently sincere inquiries after the cause of my sorrow have led me to go to the root of the matter, and I could not stop short of the development contained in this letter. It is with pain, not in anger, that I send it; hoping that you may be induced to review the whole course, of which this is only a stage, before God. If this grace were granted you, oh! how joyfully should I bury all the past, and again have sweet and tender fellowship with my beloved Son, as of old.

How sadly familiar the ground of Gosse's animadversion still seems to me, although expressed with a stylish fluency, ('the thoughtful heathen', 'Plato', 'the mute phenomena') hardly within the competence of the brethren I used to know. On the central question, however, Philip Gosse would have been as one with Mr Moses Bartholomew and Mr Gibson Stevenson: 'Thou shalt not question the Divine Oracle from the standpoint of poor, human, finite, fallen reason.' By those brethren even the most tentative inquisition (for example, how do we *know* that the Bible is the revealed word of God?) would first, and kindly, be answered by the most unashamed question-begging: 'What does the Bible say? The Bible itself *tells* us that "All scripture is given by inspiration of God" (2 Timothy 3:16).' Since the Divine Oracle itself testified to the divinity of the oracle there was nothing more that could be usefully said. Because the Holy Scriptures were an authoritative chart, the brethren could *know* and any contrary opinion would be, as Philip Gosse points out, only guesswork. Consequently, any further questioning of the verbal inspiration of all Scripture would be looked at with increasingly tight-lipped disapproval, as evidence not of honest doubt but of wilful, insolent infidelity. So it was with all the questions which increasingly preoccupied me. They were out-sider questions that, confronting the Divine Oracle, presup-posed no common ground, rather than the insider questions that were our proper study, the only questions the brethren were prepared to countenance at their weekly Bible Readings.

For example, the brethren would bother themselves about what should be the stance of the Christian with respect to law under the new dispensation of faith. What did the great apostle mean when he said that the law was a schoolmaster to bring us to Christ, but that after faith is come we are no longer under the schoolmaster (Galatians 3:24–5)? Was this a licence for the Chris-tian to behave in any old way? On the whole, the brethren thought not. 'What shall we say then? Shall we continue in sin that grace may abound? God forbid' (Romans 6:1–2).

Or take the Gospel According to Matthew chapter 16, verses 15 to 18, a typical object of brethren exegesis.

He saith unto them ... whom say ye that I am? And Simon Peter answered and said, Thou art the Christ, the Son of the living God.

161

> And Jesus answered and said unto him, Blessed art thou, Simon
> Bar-jona: for flesh and blood hath not revealed it unto thee, but
> my Father which is in heaven. And I say unto thee, That thou art
> Peter, and upon this rock I will build my church; and the gates of
> hell shall not prevail against it.

At our conversational Bible Reading, Mr Gibson Stevenson, affecting not to know the answer, would ask Mr Moses Bartholomew, who had the Greek and carried a Greek New Testament to prove it, whether this passage gave any warrant to the false conclusion drawn by the Roman Catholic Church (so-called) that Simon Peter (a mere man) was the Rock upon which Christ had promised to build His church. Not at all, Mr Bartholomew would explain to the assembled saints at the Bible Reading (Tuesdays at eight, in the will of the Lord) who had heard it all many times before. Jesus Christ gave Simon the name Peter, and if we looked at the original Greek we would see that Peter was the word for a stone and the word for rock was quite different. By the words 'this rock', Christ was referring to Simon's confession of faith, 'Thou art the Christ, the Son of the living God.' Peter himself was no more than a stone in that church, a living stone just like Mr Bleaney, and a crumb of comfort would be nudged kindly, but condescendingly, in the direction of the doubter. If we would turn to the Gospel According to John chapter 1 and verse 42, there we would read that when Andrew brought his brother Simon to our Lord, Jesus said, 'Thou art Simon the son of Jona: thou shalt be called Cephas, which is by interpretation, A stone.' So really, Mr Bartholomew, you would say there was some play on the words here, that Christ was saying, you, Simon Bar-jona, are a *stone* in my church which I am going to build on this great *rock* which is the truth which you have just now confessed that I, Jesus Christ, am the Son of God? Quite so, Mr Stevenson.

The brethren worried (a bit) about providence, free will and the absolute foreknowledge of God, especially on those occasions when Mr Bleaney took it into his head that he was probably not saved and indeed never would and never could be saved since he had never been elected in the first place. 'And we know that all things work together for good to them that love God, to them who are the called according to his purpose. For whom he did foreknow, he also did predestinate to be conformed to the image of his Son ...' (Romans 8:28–9). It was surely a sobering thought that one might not have been called, foreknown or predestinated to be conformed to Christ's image. On the whole, the brethren espoused a libertarian rather than a deterministic or Calvinistic metaphysics, but they did recognise a problem. Mr Bartholomew said he had once heard the great evangelist Dr Matthews, who would be remembered by some of the older brethren, put it like this. When we go in through the gates of heaven, we will see, written over the lintel, the words of the Book of Revelation, chapter 22 and verse 17, '... let him that is athirst come. And whosoever will, let him take the water of life freely'. Then, when we are safe inside, home at last, and we turn round, we will see written on the inner porch the words of the apostle Paul to the Ephesians, chapter 1 and verse 4, 'Chosen in him, before the foundation of the world.' The brethren, having heard it often, were quite familiar with Mr Bartholomew's compatibilist response, but they always liked to hear it again. 'Ah!' said Mr Gibson Stevenson, 'That's it! Chosen, but whosoever will!'

I cared little whether Simon Bar-jona was a stone or a rock. The questions which I would have proposed were of a different order, outsider questions which did not acknowledge a common ground. Take, for example, the proposition that God answers prayer, which was asserted by the brethren with such frequency as almost to suggest that they did not fully believe it. The proposition was, I proposed (to myself), unfalsifiable, since the protasis of every request, 'if it be Thy will', meant that whatever the outcome, God had answered our prayer. Thus, prayer for benign harvest weather (and the brethren were far from considering themselves superior to artless supplications like that) was answered equally by an Indian summer and by the worst September since records began.

In the brethren's favour it may be said that had they been seriously confronted by a dilemma of this kind, they would have been loth to accept the answer of some clever philosophers of religion, that the point of 'Thy will be done' is to acknowledge the believer's status as a contingent being in an uncertain universe, to whom all the amenities of the world are a grace of fate (or God). For the God of the brethren was, to use Carnap's distinction, the God of mythology, rather than the God of metaphysics. They believed that prayer changes things, and did not mean by that merely that prayer reconciles the believer to his own helplessness in the face of unknown and unknowable outcomes. Prayer that a mountain should be removed and cast into the sea or prayer to rescue the perishing inside, and the harvest outside Sam Mawhinney's tent *would* be answered if we prayed in the right way (with faith) and, of course, always provided that it was in the will of the Lord.

The brethren were strongly conservative on most social questions. They were supportive of corporal punishment – 'He that spareth his rod hateth his son ...' (Proverbs 13:24) – and capital punishment – 'He that smiteth a man, so that he die, shall be surely put to death' (Exodus 21:12). But the verses immediately following stipulate the death penalty for smiting father or mother, for cursing father or mother, and for kidnapping. Not far away are verses proposing the same punishment for adulterers and adulteresses and witches. Did the brethren agree? Some of the brethren I am sure did agree, and would have thought the unavailability of the sanction against swearing at your mother just another sad sign of the permissive times in which we lived, the 'last days' when men 'will not endure sound doctrine; but after their own lusts shall ... heap to themselves teachers, having

164

itching ears' (2 Timothy 4:3). But others were uncomfortable. On the one hand, they could never say that the commands of God were in any way relative to places and times. And on the other hand what could they say?

To the brethren, the Old and the New Testaments together composed a seamless unity. There was no question of regarding the latter as being in any way corrective of the former. They would not have agreed with Francis Bacon that 'prosperity is the blessing of the Old Testament and adversity is the blessing of the New'. Of a well-to-do businessman who traded honestly and gave of his income generously (a tithe) to the Lord's work at home and in foreign lands, they would remark, approvingly, 'Thus saith the Lord, "them that honour me, I will honour"' (1 Samuel 2:30). The businessman was doing well by doing good. Shortly after my father's death one brother indeed went rather beyond the bounds of propriety or at least of good taste in suggesting to my mother that since my father had conspicuously failed to prosper, there may have been some secret sin in his life and that he had been cut down in his prime because he was cumbering the ground (Luke 13:7).

According to the brethren, Jesus had not come to turn everything upside down; he had not come to destroy the law or the prophets, but to fulfil them (Matthew 5:17). But surely when Jesus said 'whosoever shall smite thee on thy right cheek, turn to him the other also' (Matthew 5:39) he was not explaining the true meaning of 'life for life, eye for eye, tooth for tooth, hand for hand, foot for foot, burning for burning, wound for wound, stripe for stripe' (Exodus 21:23–5)? Or perhaps he was (though I never heard the brethren argue it that way), and both Solomon, in Proverbs, and Paul, in the Epistle to the Romans had got it right, thus uniting the Testaments, when they proposed that there are more ways of killing a cat than drowning it in butter; '... if thine enemy hunger, feed him: if he thirst, give him drink: for in so doing thou shalt heap coals of fire on his head' (Proverbs 25:21–2, Romans 12:20).

The Old Testament seemed to be packed with examples of the material which provoked Randolph Churchill, when for a £10 bet with Evelyn Waugh he was attempting to read the Bible in a fortnight, to exclaim at frequent intervals 'God, isn't God a shit.' When, as recorded in the Second Book of Kings, the prophet Elisha was leaving Jericho for Bethel, 'there came forth little children from the city, and mocked him, and said unto him, Go up, thou bald head; go up, thou bald head. And he turned back, and looked on them, and cursed them in the name of the Lord. And there came forth two she bears out of the wood, and tare forty and two children of them.' Certainly, the children were rude, but did not a loving God's punishment seem a shade excessive? I once heard Mr Bartholomew explain that 'little children' would be better translated as 'young men'. This attempt to adjust upwards the age of responsibility was indicative of some concern on his part, since when the brethren claimed that every word of Scripture was literally the inspired word of God they meant every word of the Authorised Version, the Lord having inspired not only all the writers from Moses to John, but also the translators on King James's committee. So Mr Bartholomew was coming close to weighing the Divine Oracle in the balance of fallen reason when he suggested that the King James Bible should have read 'young men' rather than 'children'. There were not amongst the brethren any counterparts of the rich dowager who protested that Matthew chapter 19 and verse 21, '... sell that thou hast, and give to the poor', was surely a bad translation, although it should be said that as far as the brethren were concerned it might as well have been a bad translation in that they were no more disposed than the dowager to take the verse seriously.

Then there was the matter of the Amalekites. 'Thus saith the Lord of hosts, I remember that which Amalek did to Israel, how he laid wait for him in the way, when he came up from Egypt. Now go and smite Amalek, and utterly destroy all that they have, and spare them not; but slay both man and woman, infant and suckling, ox and sheep, camel and ass' (1 Samuel 15:2–3). Saul does as he is told ... almost. He smites the Amalekites, men, women, infants and sucklings, and spares only Agag the king (dog does not eat dog, or, better – Randolph Churchill again – son of a bitch does not eat son of a bitch) and the best of the sheep and of the oxen and of the fatlings and the lambs. The Lord is angry, nor is he placated by Saul's explanation that he spared the livestock only because he wanted to sacrifice them to the Lord at Gilgal. As God tells Saul through his prophet Samuel, 'Hath the Lord as great delight in burnt offerings and sacrifices, as in obeying the voice of the Lord? Behold, to obey is better than sacrifice, and to hearken than the fat of rams.' And what of Agag? Samuel, made of sterner stuff than Saul, sends for him. 'And Agag came unto him delicately. And Agag said, Surely the bitterness of death is past. And Samuel said, As thy sword hath made women childless, so shall thy mother be childless among women. And Samuel hewed Agag in pieces before the Lord in Gilgal' (1 Samuel 15:32–3).

The brethren did not run away from this passage; on the contrary, it was for them a not infrequent topic for exposition: there were lessons to be learned. The Amalekites were, they would explain, a type – a type of the flesh – and the moral of this story was that it was the Lord's wish that the young Christian should slay all fleshly or worldly desires as resolutely as Saul slew the Amalekites, or rather more so. But these were real, flesh-and-blood, suffering women and children! Surely a good and merciful God would not have commanded such a massacre just to point up the analogy that the young Christian, in 1948, should eschew such carnal pleasures as Laurence Olivier, Joan Fontaine and George Sanders in *Rebecca*? Well, so one might think, but only if one set up poor, frail, finite, human reason in competition with the Divine Oracle. God *had* so to act in order to show us just how sinful the pictures were, just how important to Him was the

167

mortification of the flesh. Sooner murder an infant in its cradle than nurse carnal desires, whether those desires were acted on or not. The desires, like the Amalekite babies, must be extirpated. So, as your boring pamphlet or tract might put it, the murder of the Amalekite babies was, from the standpoint of the Divine Oracle, a necessary murder. To question any of this was to depart from the common ground and weigh God in the balance of fallen reason.

So much for the pride of life, my undoing as it was Gosse's. What of Satan's second string, the Amalekite lust of the flesh?

'It is difficult,' writes Patricia Beer, 'to say what the brethren thought about sex.' I am not so sure. I was certainly convinced that they were against it, and that fornication came as near to being the sin against the Holy Ghost as made no difference.

On the Lord's Day following my baptism, on the very morning I came into the meeting and was for the first time privileged to break bread with the Lord's people, Livingstone Mulholland was read out. 'Read out' was our phrase for 'excommunicated', and the ground for Livingstone's expulsion was that his as yet unwed fiancée was with child. This, my first experience of the ritual, was, I gathered from my elders, a uniquely embarrassing occasion.

In accordance with settled practice, Livingstone had already been interviewed by the oversight, confronted by and convicted of his sin, and told that on the following Lord's Day he would be read out. The actual reading out did not take place until the end of the morning meeting, after the breaking of bread, since it would of course have been inappropriate for the brethren to concern themselves at an earlier stage with such distasteful goings-on, when their minds should have been concentrated on remembering the atoning work of Calvary when Jesus had died for that very Livingstone Mulholland who was now crucifying Him afresh (Hebrews 6:6). Having been interviewed and convicted, the miscreant was as good as out and no offender in living memory had come along and availed himself of a last supper on the technicality that he was not out until he had been actually read out, after we had remembered the Lord. However, the chutzpah which Livingstone had demonstrated over the years, a milkman dressed up like a solicitor or a consultant, raising the hymns and switching the tunes, sustained him to the bitter end when, bold as brass (as the brethren said), he turned up for his last morning meeting and actually gave out a hymn. The elders did not know where to look. They could not, without behaving themselves unseemly (1 Corinthians 13:5) have strongarmed him out of the hall. And so, sheepishly, we sang the fornicator's hymn, which he had the grace not to raise himself. After the closing prayer he got up, sneered at us and let himself out, not caring to stay for the formalities.

When Livingstone had gone, Mr Bartholomew asked us to open our bibles at the First Epistle to the Thessalonians, chapter 4, beginning to read at verse 2. 'For ye know what commandments we gave you by the Lord Jesus. For this is the will of God, even your sanctification, that ye should abstain from fornication; that every one of you should know how to possess his vessel in sanctification and honour; Not in the lust of concupiscence, even as the Gentiles which know not God.' I thought of the previous winter in Strabane and Maureen's breasts as firm as windfalls. Did I really know how to possess my vessel in sanctification and honour? And, if not, was I a gatecrasher at the Lord's supper (Ormo pan and Wincarnis) just concluded? One who, having eaten this bread and drunk this cup unworthily, was guilty of the body and blood of the Lord? 'But let a man examine himself, and so let him eat of that bread, and drink of that cup. For he that eateth and drinketh unworthily, eateth and drinketh damnation to himself, not discerning the Lord's body' (1 Corinthians 11:28–9). It was 1946, some two or three years before *The Heart of the Matter* and Scobie. Otherwise I would surely have been indulging myself with some romantic thoughts about the pale papery taste of the eternal sentence on my tongue.

Readings-out were not pleasant but this one was at least memorable, and the brethren did not soon forget or forgive Livingstone's nerve in showing up to break bread with decent brothers and sisters who knew how to possess their vessels.

My mother, it may be said, less quixotic than Philip Gosse, at one time saw it as her duty to find out something of my attitude towards fleshly lust. When I went away to boarding school in the autumn of 1942, she gave me a copy of a book called *What a Young Boy Ought to Know*. Some years later she gave me *What a Young Man Ought to Know*. Somewhere in between, while I pushed her in her wheelchair on one of our long, lonely walks along the towpath from the locks at Stranmillis to Shaw's Bridge through the sad December woods, she asked me if the other boys in the dormitory told dirty stories. She only asked, she said, because she believed that if a boy could feel free to tell his mother everything he would thereby remain pure in mind and spirit. This appalling advice may, for all I remember, be found in one of those shilling shockers. So did they?

I replied that they did, and she asked for examples. Well, I said, trying to think of something fairly anodyne, there was this GI who was stationed in Ballymena, and one day he asked one of the locals, 'Say! Bo! what do you do here about sex?' and the local replied 'We usually have our tay about sex.' I had the feeling that my mother knew there was more than that to dirty jokes after lights-out. Was there anything else? GI jokes were popular that term, so I told her the one about the encounter with the prostitute ('Are you free, honey?' 'No, but I'm reasonable.'). Was there anything else? My other GI joke about the Parisian in the *pissoir* who could not disguise his interest in the serviceman's cock ('Say! Bo!' 'C'est beau?' 'C'est magnifique!') was not available since my mother did not understand French. Was that all?

Well ... Why did I go on? Why did I not say that that was it? Was it simply a matter of confiding in her in my own spiritual interest? I rather think not. If my mother's interest was prurient,

170

it seems to me that my response was not entirely innocent. So, half ashamed and half excited, I told her the one about the GI who was travelling to the Red Top Inn. 'Say! Bo! How far is the Red Top Inn?' he asks the man lying with his girl in the grass. 'None of your business,' he is told. I sniggered. My mother sighed and I was glad that, since I was pushing her wheelchair, we were not face to face. Are there any more, asked my mother, persevering in her painful duty. Well, last week Marshall said that he knew a nice girl who didn't smoke and who didn't drink and who only swore if it slipped out. 'Actually, I don't get that,' I said, 'actually.' If my mother got it, she didn't explain, and there the matter rested for the time being.

She was probably right to be suspicious, both then and later, for I should say that in my case and unlike my hero, both the lust of the flesh and the pride of life played their part, first in leading me to question (with, initially, a great deal of trepidation) my status as a saved sinner, and later in convincing me that I had none.

Staying with my mother at a guesthouse in Newcastle on one of our cold, out-of-season Easter holidays, I met a young, newly married German woman, awaiting the demobilisation of her British sergeant. She was amiable, asked to see photographs of my 'girlfriend', and I found myself fantasising an invitation to her bedroom, 'Komm after twelve o'clock.' The fantasy was well developed before I recognised it as something totally at odds with the life and conduct of a born-again Christian. I think of this absurd episode only because I remember it as the first time I entertained not only the serious possibility that I was not saved, but also the thought, initially much more shocking, that I did not much care whether I was or not. In this respect, the fantasy seems to have been more potent than arrogant 'pride of life' doubts about the efficacy of prayer and the benevolence of the Old Testament God, or the suspicion that the king of the north and the king of the south were the long-departed warlords of desert tribes rather than the presidents of twentieth-century super-powers.

In London some months later, chaste and chaser, as the poet has put it so beautifully, I discovered that without a fair amount of money the way of the transgressor is hard (Proverbs 13:15). Then on a grey Sunday evening, at just about the time when the gospel meetings would be letting out all over Belfast, I came across Betty, loitering in the deserted entrance to the Piccadilly Theatre, pale, free and reasonable. By the side of the Regent Palace Hotel a taxi stood, throbbing, waiting, not unlike the human engine, I thought. 'That'll be thirty shillings dear, a quid for me and ten bob for the driver.' And seeing that it was a soft September night, the driver curled out of Piccadilly Circus, through Leicester Square, Trafalgar Square and the Admiralty Arch into the twilight of St James's Park. And so, on the broad back seat of a black taxi, on top of a plump tart with a Michelin, while crepuscular London bowed the other way and the trees in the Mall went sha sha sha, I concluded that I was just about as unsaved as it was possible to be, the Prince of Darkness, Modo and Mahu himself, contributing the *coup de grâce* by insinuating the rider that it did not, literally, matter a damn. Not many months later, back in Sunshine Street and at about the same time of day, I very nearly misled young Malcolm Bleaney to Christ.

But that was in another country, the past, where we did things differently. The saints who used to worship in the Victoria Memorial Hall in central Belfast, even then catering for the socially ambitious, have long since moved out towards the suburbs where they have acquired a large one-time Presbyterian 'church' near the university, complete with steeple, pulpit and piped organ. This 'church' they are now happy to call a church, the name, Crescent Church, unashamedly there for all to see on the front lintel. The saints of yesteryear knew better than that. For them it was worldly solecism to refer to a mere building, made of bricks and mortar, as a church. The church, whether the church universal or the local church at Pergamos or Philadelphia, at Smyrna or Sunshine Street, was the body or part of the body of all born-again believers, the bride of Christ. It if was a building, it was a house not made with hands. If there were bricks, they were the saints themselves, lively stones like Mr Bartholomew and somewhat less lively stones like Mr Bleaney composing a spiritual house, Christ, the stone which the builders disallowed being made the head of the corner (1 Peter 2:5–7). Now it seems that at least some of the brethren have joined the world, going to church on Sunday morning. Had these advances taken place forty years ago, I could with a good conscience have asked my housemaster for permission to go to church rather than, shamefaced but scrupulous, to meeting.

Inside the Crescent Church it is very grand: there are fixed pews and a gallery; there is stained glass and on the walls there

173

are no gospel texts crudely painted on *trompe-l'œil* scrolls. The preacher, who seems, like Gosse's father, to have almost the status of a pastor towards this flock, speaks with a mid-Atlantic accent and clearly sees himself in the Billy Graham mould as something of a tarmac evangelist. His sermon begins, 'Seven miles up in a Pan Am jumbo jet, I was on my way to South Korea. I was reading my Bible. The young lady sitting next to me said, "Excuse me sir, I couldn't help noticing what you are reading." ' It is his *entrée*, and in no time he is preaching Christ crucified to a glamorous but deeply dissatisfied top executive of an international food company. He speaks (to us, not to her) of Scott Fitzgerald, referring to *Tender is the Night* which has recently been televised, speaking as one who assumes that we have all seen it. Have we? Have they? Fitzgerald apparently wrote 'beautiful prose' but nevertheless died youngish of drink and despair because he too, like the food executive, did not know Jesus Christ. The reference strikes me as odd. What is Scott Fitzgerald to the brethren or the brethren to Scott Fitzgerald that he should go on so. The brethren of my youth would have known nothing of Scott Fitzgerald and would have cared less. 'All novelists are in hell' (Revelation 22:15). But this speaker seems happy to claim a nodding acquaintance, and if he condescends to the writer it is not because he is in hell with Shakespeare for all his beautiful prose but only because he was unhappy through not knowing Jesus. Pressed about hell, I imagine that he would, like Philip Gosse, appeal to the uncovenanted mercies of God which are not revealed to us. Perhaps between the stirrup and the ground Fitzgerald sought and obtained mercy.

The audience is large and surprisingly youthful. Not a few of the women wear lipstick but very few wear a hat. Whatever has happened to 1 Corinthians chapter 11 and verse 5? 'But every woman that prayeth or prophesieth with her head uncovered dishonoureth her head ...'? Judge for yourself, I think. Is it comely that a woman pray unto God uncovered?

174

In the prayers themselves, God is addressed familiarly as 'You', 'We thank You Lord for sending Your Son Jesus Christ our Saviour to die for our sins on the cross' and so on. I take it that the Y's are upper-case but it is hard to be sure. The modish cheek with which the brethren now *vouvoyer* their maker has obviously been learnt from the world, for it is a custom I have for some time been familiar with on television. I remember forty years ago a young brother who at a Bible Reading suggested that it seemed a bit artificial to speak to God calling Him 'Thee' and 'Thou'. At that time such a preposterous interjection must have come perilously close to questioning the Divine Oracle. But the young brother was treated gently and it was pointed out to him that nowhere in Scripture was Jesus or God addressed in the second-person plural. That no one else in the whole of Scripture, neither Abraham nor Satan nor Simon Bar-jona nor Nebuchadnezzar nor Eliphaz the Temanite nor the woman at the well nor the repentant thief nor Jael the wife of Heber the Kenite was ever called 'you' was not remarked on.

The singing is enthusiastic and supported not only by the organ but also by a piano. I hear that this richness is sometimes supplemented by an accordion and an electric guitar, perhaps on occasion by sackbut and timbrel. The gallery sings on its own and then the ground floor is asked to do better. The men sing against the women, the over-forties against the under-forties. Elmer Gantry might be in town. The tunes are as ever, chirpy or sentimental. Some of them are new to me. A sentimental one goes like this:

> And because He lives, I can face tomorrow,
> Because He lives, all fears are gone,
> And life is worth the living, just because He lives.

This lyric is said by the preacher, who is not old, to be a special favourite with the young people. And so it seems to be. There is something rather shameful about handsome, well-dressed young men and women, their thoughts directed to neither God nor nation but each to each, and to the back seat of a Marina, pretending to themselves so self-indulgently that if Christ was not risen from the dead they would go home and put their head in the gas oven. After three goes of this, young men and their girlfriends taking alternate lines, gallery versus floor etc., I will confess to feeling a bit faint.

It would be wrong however to infer from these capers that the brethren no longer exist in the form that was familiar to Gosse and me. Certainly the church and the world are not, at the Crescent, walking as far apart as they ought to be. But although, like Gosse, I have had neither the courage nor the energy to research the matter, unlike Gosse I do not conclude that what I have written is a *document*, an account of religious conditions which having passed away will never return. On the contrary, I am sure that the Crescent Church is the exception and that one would not have to travel as far as the mists of Augher and Clogher to discover assemblies of the Lord's people who keep to the old paths, peculiar people who would never be mistaken for evangelical Presbyterians, preserving the integrity of their quarrel with even such lookalikes (as it might seem to the world) as the Baptists and Mr Billy Graham, where the singing will be unaccompanied and God will be 'Thou' and the women will not dishonour their head and a meeting house (however ornate) could never be a church and the name of F. Scott Fitzgerald will be unheard-of.

Outside the Crescent Church, from time to time, I see wedding parties being photographed in the porch, a red carpet running from the steps to the cars. Not only is there a steeple, but the steeple contains a bell. This is really a mistake, for on the principle of 'waste not want not' the brethren cannot resist the temptation to use it on these occasions. Alas, it is a knell, evocative of the yew trees and yellow November twilights of Hammer productions long ago. As it bongs away, every sound deader than the final stroke of nine at St Mary Woolnoth, the bridegroom looks as if he at least has no need to send to know for whom it tolls. If I happen to be on foot I stop, a boat, in Fitzgerald's beautiful prose, against the current, drawn ceaselessly back into the past. Sometimes I see a familiar face, more often not.

OTHER TITLES

from

BLACKSTAFF PRESS

DUTCH INTERIOR
FRANK O'CONNOR

'Moonlight streamed down in a narrow cone and expanded in a corner of the whitewashed wall. Ned tossed restlessly and drew his hands through his hair ...

"Bloody old fools!" he whispered savagely. "Fear is the one thing in their lives – fear, fear, fear. Fear of this world or fear of the next. 'What'll become of us?' 'What'll the neighbours say?' 'You can't do this and you can't do that.' " '

Intimate and truthful, Frank O'Connor's portrayal of Irish provincial life has made him one of the most influential and respected of modern writers. But it was this same searching honesty that caused the censorship of his work by the Irish government in the 1940s and 1950s.

Banned on its publication in 1940, *Dutch Interior* is striking for the integrity of its account of the effects of Catholic conservatism and sexual repression on a group of young men and women growing up in Cork city. As they fall in love, marry, emigrate or become trapped by their own pasts, O'Connor traces their changing fortunes with characteristic humour and sensitivity. And in its insight into the 'flash points of human experience', this novel is a forceful reminder of his unique talent.

'Every word has to be read.'
New Republic

'Frank O'Connor is a master of prose.'
Irish Times

198 x 129 mm; 304 pp; 0-85640-432-2; pb;

£4.95

THE SAINT AND MARY KATE

FRANK O'CONNOR

Sharing the hardships of life in a Cork slum tenement, Mary Kate McCormick and Phil 'the Saint' Dinan become firm childhood friends. The years pass, and Phil lives up to his nickname by becoming excessively pious; meanwhile Mary Kate blossoms into a passionate young woman. And then things start to get a little complicated – for Mary Kate has more than friendship in mind …

Delightful in its account of the vagaries of unrequited love, Frank O'Connor's *The Saint and Mary Kate* is a touching study of friendship and an engaging look at the struggle between the world of the spirit and the world of the flesh.

'O'Connor is a serious artist and observer'
Irish Times

198 x 129 mm; 304 pp; 0-85640-445-4; pb

£4.95

HONOUR THY FATHER

EAMONN MC GRATH

'We walked back silently in the still evening. Already the first dew was light on the grass, moistening our toecaps to dullness. There was a new easiness between us, an understanding that had no need of words to define and circumscribe it. Inside me, rising like a lark on a bright pillar of air, my spirits soared and sang. The sky out over the islands was still warm with memory of day. A croak of crows, tumbling home to roost, passed overhead, buoyant in the free drift of air. And, over all, the elemental singing in my head. My father had recognised my individuality, my right to be myself, to carve my own destiny out of the unique piece of life that was me.'

Set in County Wexford, *Honour Thy Father* is a graceful and honest study of a growing child's experience of Irish rural life. Mc Grath explores familiar subject material – a loveless marriage, provincial small-mindedness, boarding school brutality, adolescent sexuality and first love – but breathes new life and vigour into it through his startling freshness of expression and insight.

Centring on the young John Foley's gradually heightening awareness of the complexities and hidden truths of family life, *Honour Thy Father* is a powerful portrait of a son's struggle for a deeper and more compassionate connection with his father.

'A study of a classic Irish boyhood ... a quiet and truthful book'
Claire Tomalin, *Observer*

'Its climate almost Dickensian, soaked in the aroma of country pubs'
Martin Levin, *New York Times*

198 x 129 mm; 256 pp; 0-85640-433-0; pb

£4.95

THE CHARNEL HOUSE
EAMONN MC GRATH

Set in Ardeevan sanatorium in the 1950s, when
tuberculosis was still a major cause of death in Ireland, *The
Charnel House* is a powerful study of the twilight existence
of the chronically and terminally ill.

Bringing together a wide and varied set of characters –
Richard Cogley and his sister Eileen, young lovers Vincent
and Lily, the eccentric Commander Barnwell, hospital joker
Arty Byrne, homosexual Phil Turner, and the embittered
Frank O'Shea – Eamonn Mc Grath charts their
relationships as they confront pain and death, creating a
deeply felt examination of the nature of suffering and the
unexpected strength of the human spirit.

198 x 129 mm; 224 pp; 0-85640-447-0; pb

£5.95

My Cousin Justin

Margaret Barrington

'As I watched my husband and my cousin, I realized
for the first time that … each was as badly
mutilated as if he had lost an arm or leg. What they
had lost was more because one could not see it. The
scars of war lay on their souls, and old wounds
ache.'

When Loulie Delahaie moves from the shelter of
her Anglo-Irish upbringing in County Donegal, and
the claustrophobic intensity of her relationship
with her cousin Justin Thorauld, she finds herself
embroiled in the merciless world of Dublin
journalism and revolutionary politics. There she is
swept into a headlong love affair with Egan
O'Doherty, a gunman on the run from
the Black and Tans.

The bitter violence of the Irish Civil War and the
dark shadows it casts over Loulie, Justin and Egan
are powerfully caught in this absorbing story of
passion and deceit.

'Seldom are landscape, atmosphere, characters made so
clear with such untroubled ease – the words flow as
easily on the pages as water.'
New York Herald Tribune

'a novel of great delicacy, beauty and subtlety'
Washington Post

198 x 129 mm; 288 pp; 0-85640-456-X; pb

£4.95

THE MIDDLE OF MY JOURNEY
JOHN BOYD

'I perceived the job of being a producer – the name itself is significant – to being a kind of midwife. You persuaded, pummelled, encouraged, pacified, pleaded, cajoled ordinary and extraordinary people to give birth to their thoughts by speaking them into a microphone.'

Appointed as a radio producer by the BBC in Belfast in 1946, John Boyd found himself at odds with the 'literary apartheid' and conservatism then governing broadcasting. But over the next twenty years, Boyd's quiet but determined work behind the scenes – bringing the voices of writers like Frank O'Connor, Louis MacNeice and Philip Larkin to a wider audience – made him one of the BBC's most influential regional producers.

Covering those years of intense activity, this second volume of autobiography from John Boyd paints a vibrant picture of creative and artistic life in Belfast.

'This man of calm and honest judgement.'
Benedict Kiely, *Irish Times*

198 x 129 mm; 240 pp; 0-85640-438-1; pb

£5.95

THE HOLLOW BALL

SAM HANNA BELL

'He should have known that McFall's subversive concern with these men who went through life as ciphers would grow and swell in the back streets. And he felt no shame in regarding himself as different from them ... He was going, by right, to where men paid honourably and handsomely for his considerable skill. He stared back coldly at the heavy face of his companion.'

Trapped in their poorly paid menial jobs in a clothing firm, David Minnis and Bonar McFall both yearn for a better life. McFall is angered by the injustice he sees around him and seeks change through radical politics; Minnis dreams of becoming a star footballer and dedicates his life to the pursuit of 'the hollow ball'. When he is signed by Glenbank Athletic, his life changes dramatically. Success breeds success, but also compromise and betrayal, gradually alienating Minnis from his family and friends.

Painting a haunting picture of working-class Belfast in the 1930s – where men and women 'fight like dogs for an extra twopence an hour' – this novel from the author of *December Bride* is a poignant study of the tragic price that is paid for fame.

'... told skilfully, calmly, and at times beautifully ... Bell has given us a vivid and accurate portrayal of working-class Protestant people.'
Brian Friel, *Irish Times*

'... has no truck with the journalese and sensationalism that often characterize fiction about sport.'
Times Literary Supplement

198 x 129 mm; 256 pp; 0-85640-452-7; pb

£4.95

DECEMBER BRIDE
SAM HANNA BELL

'a story of the eternal triangle, held, like the land, by
stubborn force'
Fortnight

THE CLASSIC NOVEL OF ULSTER LIFE, NOW A MAJOR FILM.

Sarah Gomartin, the servant girl on Andrew Echlin's farm,
bears a child to one of Andrew's sons. But which one? Her
steadfast refusal over many years to 'bend and contrive
things' by choosing one of the brothers reverberates
through the puritan Ulster community, alienating clergy
and neighbours, hastening her mother's death and casting
a cold shadow on the life of her children.

December Bride, directed by Thaddeus O'Sullivan and
starring Saskia Reeves, Donal McCann and Ciaran Hinds,
was ecstatically received at its première at the 1990
Dublin Film Festival.

'not just a remarkable artistic achievement, but also a remarkable
political one ... opens up a community's sense of itself, restoring
a richness and complexity to a history that has been deliberately
narrowed'
Fintan O'Toole, *Irish Times*, reviewing
the film *December Bride*

198 x 129 mm; 304 pp; 0-85640-061-0; pb

£4.95

CASTLE CORNER

JOYCE CARY

'The crowd, now gathered close, watched in silence the bailiffs fetch rakes, poles, and a long-handled pruning hook, but when they approached Con's new-built cabin and began to hook down the roof, there were sudden yells of "Give them Martin, up the League."

'Martin was a district inspector of police murdered the year before.

'Old John gazed round with an air of mild reproach; John Chass, looking embarrassed, smiled and attempted a joke; the D.I., with a marble face but very brisk legs, walked up and down in front of the police, who looked like men awaiting the dentist, some with resignation, some with ferocious resolution.'

Violent evictions in Donegal, fashionable drawing-rooms in London, compromise and degradation in a West African trading station – Joyce Cary's panoramic novel follows the fortunes of the Anglo-Irish Corner family as they contend with a changing world at the century's turn.

'Mr Cary's book is stupendous ... There is an intellectual richness ... pages of allusive anecdote, chat, picture, narrative, family history, and a grim display of human squalor ... It is a grand effect; and the book has a fury of incontrovertible detail.'
Frank Swinnerton, *Observer*

198 x 129 mm; 432 pp; 0-85640-422-5; pb

£5.95

ORDERING BLACKSTAFF BOOKS

All Blackstaff Press books are available through bookshops. In the case of difficulty, however, orders can be made directly to the publisher. Indicate clearly the title and number of copies required and send order with your name and address to:

CASH SALES

Blackstaff Press Limited
3 Galway Park
Dundonald
Belfast BT16 0AN
Northern Ireland

Please enclose a remittance to the value of the cover price plus: £1.00 for the first book plus 60p per copy for each additional book ordered to cover postage and packing. Payment should be made in sterling by UK personal cheque, postal order, sterling draft or international money order, made payable to Blackstaff Press Limited.

Applicable only in the UK and Republic of Ireland
Full catalogue available on request